AF407252

CONTENTS

THE ART OF CODE

◆ ◆ ◆

BY SAM STEED

◆ ◆ ◆

Exploring the World Of Programming Languages

"The Art of Code: Exploring the World of Programming Languages"

Description:

"The Art of Code" is a comprehensive and engaging exploration of programming languages, designed to provide readers with a solid foundation in the art and science of computer programming. This book is perfect for beginners who are curious about coding, as well as seasoned programmers looking to expand their knowledge and explore new languages.

Key Features:

1. Introduction to Programming:

- Demystifying the world of programming and its importance in today's digital age.

- Understanding the fundamentals of algorithms, data structures, and problem-solving.

2. Exploring Popular Programming Languages:

- A detailed examination of popular languages like Python, JavaScript, Java, C++, and more.

- Each language is presented in a structured and accessible manner, covering syntax, features, and best practices.

- Hands-on exercises and coding examples to reinforce learning.

3. Language Design and Paradigms:

- Exploring different programming paradigms, including procedural, object-oriented, functional, and declarative.

- Understanding how language design choices impact coding styles and problem-solving approaches.

4. Building Real-World Applications:

- Practical examples and case studies that demonstrate the power and versatility of each programming language.

- Building applications such as web development, mobile apps, data analysis, and automation.

5. Comparative Analysis:

- A side-by-side comparison of programming languages, highlighting their strengths, weaknesses, and ideal use cases.

- Helping readers make informed decisions when choosing the right language for a specific project.

6. Emerging Trends and Future of Programming:

- Exploring emerging languages and trends in the programming landscape, such as machine learning, blockchain, and the Internet of Things (IoT).

- Discussing the evolving role of programmers and the importance of continuous learning.

7. Best Practices and Resources:

- Proven coding practices, tips, and techniques for writing clean, efficient, and maintainable code.

- Recommended resources, including books, online tutorials, and communities for further learning and growth.

"The Art of Code" is not just a technical guide but a captivating journey into the world of programming languages. It equips readers with the knowledge and skills needed to express their creativity, solve complex problems, and bring their ideas to life through the power of code. Whether you're an aspiring programmer or an experienced developer, this book will inspire and empower you to master the art of programming languages.

Demystifying the world of programming and its importance in today's digital age.

Programming has become an essential skill in today's digital age, permeating almost every aspect of modern society. From healthcare and finance to retail and entertainment, technology is rapidly transforming industries across the globe, and with it comes the need for skilled programmers. Yet, for many people, the world of programming can seem daunting, leading to misconceptions and a lack of understanding about its importance. In this article, we aim to demystify programming and shed light on why it is essential in today's technologically-driven world. We'll cover the basics of programming, its impact on various industries, and the benefits of learning to code, as well as explore trends and innovations that are shaping the future of programming.

1. Introduction: Understanding Programming in Today's Digital Age

What is Programming?

Programming is the process of designing, writing, and testing computer programs. A program is a set of instructions that tells a computer what to do and how to do it. These instructions can be written in a variety of programming languages, each with its syntax and rules.

Why is Programming Important Today?

Programming has become essential in today's digital age, as it is the foundation of everything from websites and mobile apps to video games and artificial intelligence systems. It has enabled us to automate processes, create new technologies, and streamline communication. In a world where technology is constantly evolving, programming skills have become highly valued and sought after by employers.

1. The Evolving Role of Programming in Modern Society

Programming's Impact on the Digital Age

Programming has been instrumental in shaping the digital age and its impact is far-reaching. It has revolutionized the way we access information, communicate, and conduct business. It has also transformed industries and created new ones, such as the app economy. With the rise of the Internet of Things (IoT), programming is becoming even more critical as everything from cars to home appliances is now becoming connected.

Programming's Influence on the Modern Workforce

Programming has also had a significant impact on the modern workforce. With the increased automation of jobs, learning to code has become a valuable skill for individuals across a wide range of industries. In addition, many companies now require programming skills for roles outside of traditional tech positions, such as marketing and finance.

1. The Benefits of Learning to Code: Personal and Professional Advantages

Developing Critical Thinking and Problem-Solving Skills

Learning to code requires logical thinking and problem-solving skills which can improve your ability to approach challenges in all aspects of life. The process of debugging errors in code can also enhance your creativity and patience.

Improved Career Prospects and New Opportunities

Programming skills can open doors to a wide range of lucrative and in-demand careers in tech, such as software development, data analysis, and cybersecurity. However, programming skills also offer new opportunities outside of traditional tech roles, such as creating your startup or freelancing as a web developer.

1. Demystifying the Basics of Programming: Common Languages and Terminology

What are Programming Languages?

Programming languages are formal languages designed to instruct computers and machines. They can be used to create software, websites, and mobile apps. Some common programming languages include JavaScript, Python, and C++.

Common Programming Terminology and Concepts

Programming has its unique jargon, which can be overwhelming to beginners. Some commonly used terms include variables, functions, loops, and conditional statements. Each of these terms refers to a specific concept that is used in programming to perform specific tasks. By gaining an understanding of these concepts, you can learn how to write code and create your programs.

1. How Programming is Transforming Different Industries

Programming has become an integral part of virtually all industries, transforming the way they operate and interact with their customers. Here are just a few examples:

Healthcare

Programmers are revolutionizing medicine with the development of electronic health records (EHRs), allowing healthcare providers to access patient data quickly. Additionally, telemedicine applications allow doctors to remotely diagnose and treat patients in real time, saving time and resources.

Finance

Programming has completely transformed the financial industry with the introduction of high-frequency trading algorithms, allowing traders to make millions of trades in seconds. Additionally, blockchain technology is revolutionizing the way financial transactions occur, making them more secure and efficient.

Retail

E-commerce websites have become prevalent, and online shopping is more popular than ever before. Thanks to programming, retailers can now offer personalized product recommendations and virtual shopping experiences to their customers.

1. The Future of Programming: Trends and Innovations to Watch Out For

As technology continues to advance, programming will continue to play a more significant role across industries. Here are some programming trends and innovations expected to shape the future:

Emerging Technologies

The emergence of new technologies such as 5G and the Internet of Things (IoT) will create opportunities for programmers to create new applications and services. For example, programmers can leverage IoT to create smart homes and cities.

Artificial Intelligence and Machine Learning

The use of artificial intelligence (AI) and machine learning (ML) is growing rapidly in the business world, and this trend is expected to continue. With the help of programming, AI and ML can be used to develop predictive models, drive automation, and enhance data analysis.

1. Conclusion: The Importance of Programming in a Technologically-Driven World

Programming has become an essential skill in today's increasingly digital world. It has revolutionized industries, created new job opportunities, and improved the way we live our lives.

Why Everyone Should Learn to Code

Learning to code is not just for programmers; it's an essential skill that everyone should have in a technologically-driven world. It teaches critical thinking, problem-solving, and creativity, which are valuable skills that can be applied to any industry. In addition, it provides a better understanding of how technology works, making us more informed and responsible citizens of the digital age. In conclusion, programming is a vital skill that is becoming increasingly important in our technology-driven world. It is a tool that can unlock incredible opportunities and transform industries. Whether you're looking to improve your career prospects or develop critical thinking skills, learning to code is an investment that will pay off in the long run. So, take the first step and explore the world of programming today!

FAQ

Why is programming important in today's digital age?

Programming is essential in today's digital age because it is the driving force behind much of the technology we use every day. From our smartphones and computers to the software that powers businesses and industries, programming is at the forefront of innovation and progress.

What are the benefits of learning to code?

Learning to code can have significant personal and professional benefits. It can improve critical thinking and problem-solving skills, open up new career opportunities, and enhance creativity and innovation. Additionally, coding is a valuable skill to have in an increasingly technology-driven job market.

Is programming difficult to learn?

Like any new skill, programming may seem difficult at first. Still, with the right resources and approach, it's a skill that anyone can learn. Many online resources and courses make learning to code accessible to beginners, and with practice, anyone can become proficient in programming.

What are some programming languages to consider learning?

There are many programming languages to consider learning, and the best language for you will depend on your specific goals and interests. Some popular languages for beginners to consider include Python, Java, and JavaScript. Ultimately, the choice of language will depend on your career aspirations and the type of projects you want to work on.

Understanding the fundamentals of algorithms, data structures, and problem-solving.

Algorithms, data structures, and problem-solving are at the heart of computer science and software engineering. These fundamental concepts are essential for designing efficient and effective software solutions to complex problems. Understanding the principles of algorithms and data structures is critical for creating robust, scalable, and high-performance applications. Effective problem-solving techniques are equally important for identifying, analyzing, and solving problems using algorithms and data structures. In this article, we will provide a comprehensive introduction to the fundamentals of algorithms, data structures, and problem-solving, exploring their key concepts, principles, and real-world applications.

INTRODUCTION TO ALGORITHMS, DATA STRUCTURES, AND PROBLEM-SOLVING

Algorithms, data structures, and problem-solving are three fundamental building blocks of computer science. Algorithms are step-by-step procedures that take inputs and produce outputs. Data structures are a way of organizing and storing data in a computer so that it can be accessed and manipulated efficiently. Problem-solving involves finding a solution to a problem using computational techniques. In this article, we will explore the basics of these three concepts and how they are used in computer science.

Why Algorithms, Data Structures, and Problem-Solving Matter

Algorithms, data structures, and problem-solving are important because they form the backbone of computer science. They are used to solve complex problems, from analyzing big data to designing computer programs and systems. Understanding these concepts is crucial for developing efficient and effective software, as well as improving overall computer performance. By mastering algorithms, data structures, and problem-solving techniques, developers and computer scientists can create innovative solutions for a wide range of applications.

ALGORITHMS: DEFINITION, TYPES, AND CLASSIFICATION

What Are Algorithms and Why Are They Important?

An algorithm is a set of instructions designed to perform a specific task. They are used in a wide range of applications, from simple calculations to complex processing systems. Algorithms are important because they allow us to efficiently solve problems and automate tasks that would otherwise be time-consuming and error-prone.

The Different Types of Algorithms

There are many different types of algorithms, including sorting algorithms, search algorithms, graph algorithms, and numerical algorithms. Sorting algorithms, as the name suggests, are used for sorting data. Search algorithms are used for finding specific data in a set of data. Graph algorithms are used for analyzing networks and relationships between data points. Numerical algorithms are used for computing mathematical functions and operations.

How Are Algorithms Classified?

Algorithms can be classified based on their complexity and the way they process data. The three primary classifications are linear, exponential, and logarithmic algorithms. Linear algorithms process data sequentially, one item at a time, and have a runtime that is proportional to the size of the input data. Exponential algorithms process data in a combinatorial fashion, which means that the runtime grows exponentially as the size of the input data increases. Logarithmic algorithms process data by dividing it into smaller and smaller pieces until a solution is found, which means that the runtime grows logarithmically as the size of the input data increases.

DATA STRUCTURES: DEFINITION, TYPES, AND IMPLEMENTATION

What Are Data Structures and Why Are They Important?

A data structure is a way of organizing and storing data in a computer so that it can be accessed and manipulated efficiently. Data structures are important because they allow us to optimize the performance of algorithms and reduce the time and resources required for processing large amounts of data.

The Different Types of Data Structures

There are many different types of data structures, including arrays, linked lists, trees, stacks, queues, and hash tables. Arrays are used for storing data in a linear fashion. Linked lists are used for storing data in a non-linear fashion. Trees are used for storing hierarchical data. Stacks and queues are used for storing data in a first-in, last-out fashion. Hash tables are used for storing data in a key-value format.

How Are Data Structures Implemented?

Data structures can be implemented using various programming languages, but they are typically implemented using classes and objects in object-oriented programming. The implementation of a data structure depends on the specific requirements of the algorithm or application in which it will be used.

PROBLEM-SOLVING TECHNIQUES: STRATEGIES AND APPROACHES

The Importance of Problem-Solving

Problem-solving is an essential skill for computer scientists and developers. It involves identifying a problem, analyzing the requirements and constraints, and developing a solution using computational techniques. Problem-solving is important because it allows us to solve complex problems and create innovative solutions.

Problem-Solving Strategies

There are many different problem-solving strategies, including trial and error, divide and conquer, backtracking, and heuristic algorithms. Trial and error involve trying different solutions until one is found that works. Divide and conquer involves breaking a problem down into smaller sub-problems and solving each one individually. Backtracking involves trying different solutions and backtracking when a solution is found to be incorrect. Heuristic algorithms involve using rules of thumb or approximation methods to find a solution.

Problem-Solving Approaches

There are two primary problem-solving approaches: analytical and creative. Analytical problem-solving involves using logical and systematic methods to solve problems. Creative problem-solving involves using intuition, imagination, and creativity to find innovative solutions. Both approaches are important for solving complex problems and developing innovative solutions.

ALGORITHM ANALYSIS: PERFORMANCE METRICS AND COMPLEXITY

The Importance of Algorithm Analysis

Algorithm analysis is the process of examining the efficiency of computer algorithms and evaluating their performance. It is a crucial aspect of software development as it helps to determine the strengths and weaknesses of an algorithm, and ultimately leads to the creation of more efficient and effective software. The importance of algorithm analysis cannot be overstated, as it enables developers to optimize their algorithms and improve the end-user experience.

Performance Metrics for Algorithms

There are various metrics used to measure the performance of algorithms. These include time complexity, space complexity, and accuracy. Time complexity measures the amount of time an algorithm takes to execute, while space complexity measures the amount of memory required by an algorithm. Accuracy refers to how well an algorithm performs its intended task.

Complexity Analysis for Algorithms

Complexity analysis is the process of analyzing the performance of an algorithm as the input size increases. It involves determining the worst-case, best-case, and average-case scenario for the algorithm, as well as its big-O notation. The big-O notation is used to describe the upper bound of an algorithm's time complexity as the input size grows.

ADVANCED TOPICS IN ALGORITHMS AND DATA STRUCTURES

Sorting Algorithms

Sorting algorithms are used to organize data in ascending or descending order. There are various sorting algorithms, including bubble sort, insertion sort, quicksort, and mergesort. Each algorithm has its advantages and disadvantages, and the choice of algorithm depends on the nature of the data and the desired outcome.

Graph Algorithms

Graph algorithms are used to solve problems related to graphs, which are data structures consisting of nodes and edges. Graph algorithms are used in a wide range of applications, including computer networking, social networks, and transportation systems. Examples of graph algorithms include depth-first search, breadth-first search, and Dijkstra's algorithm.

Dynamic Programming

Dynamic programming is a method of solving problems by breaking them down into smaller, simpler sub-problems. It is often used in optimization problems, where the goal is to find the best or optimal solution. Dynamic programming is also used in a variety of applications, including computer graphics, bioinformatics, and economics.

REAL-WORLD APPLICATIONS OF ALGORITHMS AND DATA STRUCTURES

Using Algorithms and Data Structures in Web Development

Algorithms and data structures play a crucial role in web development. For example, search engines use algorithms to index and search through web pages, while social media platforms use data structures to store and retrieve user data. Additionally, web developers use sorting algorithms to organize data, and graph algorithms to optimize website performance.

Using Algorithms and Data Structures in Machine Learning

Machine learning is an area of computer science that uses algorithms and statistical models to enable computers to learn from data. Algorithms and data structures are used extensively in machine learning, including decision trees, neural networks, and support vector machines. These algorithms are used to analyze and make predictions based on large volumes of data.

Using Algorithms and Data Structures in Computer Networking

Algorithms and data structures are also important in computer networking, where they are used to optimize network performance and reliability. For example, routing algorithms are used to determine the most efficient path between two nodes, while data structures are used to organize and process network traffic.

BEST PRACTICES FOR EFFECTIVE ALGORITHMIC PROBLEM-SOLVING

Understand the Problem

The first step in effective algorithmic problem-solving is to fully understand the problem at hand. This involves breaking down the problem into smaller, simpler sub-problems and identifying the key requirements and constraints.

Choose the Right Algorithm and Data Structure

Once the problem has been fully understood, the next step is to choose the most appropriate algorithm and data structure. This involves evaluating the strengths and weaknesses of different algorithms and data structures and selecting the one that is best suited for the problem at hand.

Test and Debug Your Solution

Finally, it is important to thoroughly test and debug the solution. This involves running the algorithm using different input values and verifying that it produces the expected output. Debugging involves identifying and fixing any errors or bugs in the code. In conclusion, understanding the basics of algorithms, data structures, and problem-solving is crucial for any software engineer or computer scientist. These concepts are the foundation of efficient and effective software design and implementation. By applying the knowledge gained from this article, you will be able to design and implement efficient algorithms, choose the right data structures, and solve complex problems in a structured and effective way. Whether you are a beginner or an experienced programmer, mastering these fundamentals is an essential step toward becoming a skilled and proficient software developer.

FAQ

What is an algorithm?

An algorithm is a set of instructions or rules that define how to solve a problem. It is a step-by-step procedure for solving a specific problem or accomplishing a specific task.

What is a data structure?

A data structure is a way of organizing and storing data in a computer program so that it can be accessed and used efficiently. It is a collection of data values, the relationships among them, and the functions or operations that can be applied to the data.

Why are algorithms and data structures important?

Algorithms and data structures are important because they are the building blocks of computer programs. They are essential for writing efficient, reliable, and scalable software solutions for various applications.

What are the best practices for algorithmic problem-solving?

The best practices for algorithmic problem-solving include understanding the problem, choosing the right algorithm and data structure, testing and debugging the solution, and optimizing the solution as needed. It is also important to consider the time and space complexity of the algorithm and data structure and to maintain good coding practices.

A detailed examination of popular languages like Python, JavaScript, Java, C++, and more.

Programming languages have become an integral part of modern-day society. In the digital age, software systems power everything from simple web applications to complex artificial intelligence algorithms. While there are hundreds of programming languages available, only a handful of them are widely used. This article will provide a detailed examination of popular programming languages like Python, JavaScript, Java, C++, and more. We will explore the features, advantages, and disadvantages of each language, compare them with others, and discuss the factors that developers should consider before choosing a language for their projects.

INTRODUCTION TO POPULAR PROGRAMMING LANGUAGES

Programming languages are the building blocks of the modern technological world. From software development to web development and beyond, programming languages are essential for creating some of the most impactful and innovative applications and tools. However, with so many programming languages being used today, it can be overwhelming to choose just one to learn. In this article, we'll examine some of the most popular programming languages, their features, advantages, and limitations.

Overview of Programming Languages

Programming languages are a set of instructions used to develop software, mobile applications, websites, and more. Just like spoken languages, different programming languages have different syntax, grammar, and rules. Some of the most popular programming languages include Java, Python, C++, JavaScript, Ruby, and PHP.

Why Study Programming Languages?

Learning programming languages can open up a world of opportunities and pave the way for a career as a software developer, web developer, data analyst, or even game developer. Knowing different programming languages can also help one choose the right tool for a given project, optimize code, and improve problem-solving skills.

PYTHON: ITS FEATURES, ADVANTAGES, AND DISADVANTAGES

Introduction to Python

Python is an easy-to-learn, high-level programming language that is popular for its simplicity and versatility. It was created by Guido van Rossum in the late 1980s and has since become one of the most popular programming languages in the world.

Features of Python

Python has a lot of features that make it an excellent choice for beginners and experienced programmers alike. With its clean syntax, built-in libraries, and dynamic typing, Python makes writing code both simple and efficient. Additionally, it supports object-oriented, functional, and procedural programming paradigms.

Advantages of Python

Python is widely used in various fields such as web development, data science, machine learning, and artificial intelligence. Its ease of use and readability make it an ideal choice for beginners, while its powerful libraries and frameworks make it a popular language for more advanced developers. Python also has a large and active community, which means that there is plenty of support and resources available for those who want to learn it.

Disadvantages of Python

While Python has a lot of advantages, it also has its drawbacks. One of the most significant limitations of Python is its execution speed compared to languages like C++ and Java. Python is also not suitable for developing low-level applications such as device drivers or operating systems.

JAVASCRIPT: ITS USES AND LIMITATIONS

Introduction to JavaScript

JavaScript is a high-level, interpreted programming language that is used to create interactive websites and web applications. It was created by Brendan Eich in the mid-1990s and has since become one of the most widely used programming languages in web development.

Uses of JavaScript

JavaScript is used for creating a variety of web-related tasks, including dynamic web pages, user interface design, and web applications. It can also be used for server-side programming with the help of Node.js.

Limitations of JavaScript

Despite its widespread use and popularity, JavaScript has some limitations. One of the most significant limitations of JavaScript is its inability to handle multi-threaded operations, making it not well suited for high-performance applications. Additionally, JavaScript can also be prone to security vulnerabilities if not properly written and tested.

JAVA: ITS STRENGTHS AND WEAKNESSES

Introduction to Java

Java is a popular, object-oriented programming language that was invented in the mid-1990s by James Gosling. With its multi-platform capabilities, Java has become one of the most popular programming languages for building software for both desktop and mobile platforms.

Strengths of Java

One of the key strengths of Java is its platform independence, which allows applications to run on different platforms without any modification. Java is also known for its robustness, reliability, and scalability. Its object-oriented approach enables developers to build complex software applications with ease.

Weaknesses of Java

Java's verbosity and steep learning curve can be a drawback for beginners. Additionally, the Java Virtual Machine, which is necessary for executing Java code, can be resource-intensive and require more memory than other programming languages.

C++: ITS HISTORY, APPLICATIONS, AND PROSPECTS

Introduction to C++

C++ is a high-performance object-oriented programming language that is widely used in developing application software, system software, and game engines. It is an extension of the C language that provides additional features such as object-oriented programming, templates, and exception handling.

History of C++

C++ was designed by Bjarne Stroustrup in 1979 as an extension of the C language. It was initially called "C with classes" and was used mainly for developing operating systems and system software. In the 1990s, C++ became popular in developing desktop applications and large-scale projects. Today, C++ is used in a wide range of applications, including game development, scientific computing, finance, and embedded systems.

Applications of C++

C++ is used in many industries such as gaming, finance, and aerospace. It is ideal for developing resource-intensive applications due to its high performance and low-level memory management capabilities. Some of the popular applications of C++ are game engines, operating systems, web browsers, machine learning frameworks, and embedded systems.

Prospects of C++

C++ has a bright future due to its unmatched performance, high scalability, and established use cases. With the increasing demand for high-performance computing and the growth of the Internet of Things (IoT), C++ is becoming more relevant than ever. It is also being used by emerging technologies such as blockchain, virtual reality, and autonomous vehicles.

COMPARISON OF POPULAR PROGRAMMING LANGUAGES

Programming Paradigms

Programming languages are classified based on their programming paradigms, which are the fundamental styles of computer programming. Some popular programming paradigms include imperative, functional, object-oriented, and procedural.

Language Syntax

The syntax of a programming language refers to the set of rules that define how the language is written and interpreted by the computer. Each programming language has its syntax, which can be simple or complex depending on the language.

Applications of Programming Languages

Different programming languages are used for different applications. For instance, Python is used for data science and machine learning, while JavaScript is used for web development. Java is used for developing enterprise applications, and C++ is used for system software, game engines, and high-performance computing.

FACTORS TO CONSIDER WHEN CHOOSING A PROGRAMMING LANGUAGE

Project Requirements

When choosing a programming language, it is essential to consider the requirements of the project. Some projects require a language that is easy to learn, while others require a language that can handle complex computations.

Developer Experience

The experience and skills of the development team should be considered when choosing a programming language. If the team is proficient in a particular language, it may be more efficient to choose a language that the team is familiar with.

Community Support

The community support behind a programming language is also crucial. A language with an active community can provide better resources, libraries, and tools that can help improve the development process.

CONCLUSION: CHOOSING THE RIGHT PROGRAMMING LANGUAGE FOR YOUR PROJECT

Summary of Key Takeaways

Choosing the right programming language is critical to the success of any project. It is important to consider the programming paradigms, syntax, and applications of different languages, as well as project requirements, developer experience, and community support.

Final Thoughts

In conclusion, there is no "one-size-fits-all" programming language. The choice of a language depends on several factors, including project requirements, developer experience, and community support. By carefully considering these factors, developers can choose the right language for their project and increase their chances of success. In conclusion, the right programming language for any project depends on several factors such as project requirements, developer experience, and community support. By understanding the features, advantages, and disadvantages of popular programming languages like Python, JavaScript, Java, C++, and others, developers can make informed decisions when choosing a language for their projects. With the right programming language, developers can create efficient and robust software systems that meet the needs of both individuals and businesses.

FAQ

What is the most popular programming language?

Currently, the most popular programming language in the world is Java. However, this can vary depending on the industry and region.

Which programming language is better for web development: Python or JavaScript?

Both Python and JavaScript have their advantages and disadvantages when it comes to web development. Python is generally better for backend development, while JavaScript excels in frontend development. Ultimately, the language you choose depends on your specific needs and the requirements of your project.

Is it better to learn multiple programming languages or focus on mastering one?

It's always a good idea to know multiple programming languages, especially if you're a beginner. However, it's generally better to focus on mastering one language before moving on to others. This way, you can become proficient in one language and have a solid understanding of programming concepts that can be applied to other languages.

What factors should I consider when choosing a programming language for my project?

When choosing a programming language, it's important to consider factors such as project requirements, developer experience, and community support. You should also consider the scalability and maintainability of the language and its compatibility with other languages and platforms.

Each language is presented in a structured and accessible manner, covering syntax, features, and best practices.

Learning a new language can be a daunting endeavor, especially when it comes to programming languages. With so many options available, it can be overwhelming to choose the right one for your project. However, learning a new language can also be incredibly rewarding and open up new opportunities for personal and professional growth. In this article, we will explore how each language is presented in a structured and accessible manner, covering syntax, features, and best practices. Whether you are a beginner or an experienced programmer, this guide will provide valuable insights and strategies for effective language learning.

INTRODUCTION: THE IMPORTANCE OF STRUCTURED AND ACCESSIBLE LANGUAGE LEARNING

The world of programming is constantly changing, and as such, it's essential to stay up to date with the latest techniques and tools. Learning a new programming language is one of the best ways to keep up with industry standards and expand your skill set.

When it comes to learning a new programming language, it's essential to have a structured and accessible approach. This article will explore the benefits and challenges of learning a new language, the building blocks of language (syntax), key features that make each language unique, and best practices for effective language learning.

The benefits of learning a new language

Learning a new programming language can bring a wealth of benefits, including:

- Increased employability: having diverse programming skills makes you more marketable to potential employers.

- Enhanced problem-solving: learning different programming languages allows you to approach problem-solving from different angles, which can enhance your critical thinking skills.

- Better understanding of different programming paradigms: learning different languages exposes you to different programming paradigms, which can help you develop a deeper understanding of how programming languages work.

The challenges of learning a new language

Learning a new programming language can be a daunting task, especially if you're not familiar with the language's syntax and features. Some of the challenges you might face include:

- Syntax: each programming language has its unique syntax rules, which can be difficult to understand initially.

- Features: different languages have different features, such as loops, functions, and data types, which can take time to master.

- Time management: learning a new language requires dedication and time commitment, which can be challenging if you have other commitments.

UNDERSTANDING SYNTAX: THE BUILDING BLOCKS OF LANGUAGE

The basics of syntax

Syntax refers to the set of rules that govern how words and symbols are arranged to create a program. Every programming language has its unique syntax rules, which can determine how effective and efficient the code is.

Some essential syntax elements include:

- Variables: used to store data.

- Operators: used to perform mathematical and logical operations.

- Control flow structures: used to control the flow of the program, such as loops and if statements.

How syntax differs across languages

Each programming language has its unique syntax rules, which can make learning a new language challenging. For instance, Python uses whitespace to delimit blocks of code, while C++ uses curly braces. Learning the syntax rules of a new language is essential to avoid syntax errors and writing efficient code.

EXPLORING FEATURES: KEY ELEMENTS THAT MAKE EACH LANGUAGE UNIQUE

The unique features of popular programming languages

Different programming languages have different features that make them unique. For instance, Python is known for its simplicity and readability, while Java is popular for its portability and security.

Other popular programming languages and their unique features include:

- C++: known for its performance and flexibility

- JavaScript: used for web development and known for its ability to run on client-side browsers

- Ruby: popular for its easy-to-read syntax and object-oriented programming capabilities

How to choose the right language for your project

Choosing the right language for your project depends on several factors, including:

- The project's requirements: some languages are better suited for specific projects, such as web development or artificial intelligence.

- Personal expertise: if you're proficient in a particular language, it might be best to stick with what you know.

- Community support: some languages have more significant community support than others, making it easier to find help and resources.

BEST PRACTICES FOR EFFECTIVE LANGUAGE LEARNING: TIPS AND STRATEGIES FOR SUCCESS

Setting achievable language learning goals

Setting achievable language learning goals is essential to stay motivated and track progress. Some tips for setting effective goals include:

- Breaking down goals into smaller, achievable tasks.

- Setting deadlines for each task.

- Celebrating each milestone achieved.

Strategies for practicing and retaining the language

To retain a new language, it's essential to practice consistently and apply the knowledge to real-life projects. Some effective strategies for practicing include:

- Building small projects that apply the language's features.

- Reading and writing code daily.

- Collaborating with other learners or experienced programmers for peer review and feedback.

In conclusion, learning a new programming language can be a challenging but rewarding experience. With a structured and accessible approach, understanding syntax, exploring unique features, and applying effective language learning strategies, you can become proficient in a new language in no time.

THE BENEFITS OF LEARNING MULTIPLE LANGUAGES: ENHANCING COGNITIVE ABILITIES AND PROFESSIONAL OPPORTUNITIES

Learning a new language not only enables you to communicate with people from different cultures but also offers significant cognitive benefits. Studies have shown that bilingual individuals have better memory, enhanced problem-solving skills, and are more creative compared to those who speak only one language.

Additionally, being multilingual can open up a world of professional opportunities. Knowing multiple languages can improve your chances of landing a job in an international company or organization, and it also provides a competitive advantage in industries such as tourism, diplomacy, and language education.

The cognitive benefits of multilingualism

Learning a new language stimulates the brain, helping to improve its cognitive abilities. Multilingualism has been linked to better memory retention, improved decision-making skills, and enhanced creativity. Being bilingual has been shown to delay the onset of age-related cognitive decline and may even help reduce the risk of developing Alzheimer's disease.

The professional advantages of being multilingual

In today's globalized world, being multilingual is becoming increasingly valuable. Companies and organizations are always looking for employees who can speak multiple languages to facilitate communication with clients or partners from different countries. Moreover, being fluent in different languages can help you stand out in a competitive job market, especially if you're interested in pursuing a career in international business, diplomacy, or translation.

OVERCOMING COMMON LANGUAGE LEARNING CHALLENGES: STRATEGIES FOR STAYING MOTIVATED AND OVERCOMING OBSTACLES

Learning a new language can be challenging, and it's common to experience frustration and setbacks. However, with a little determination and some helpful strategies, you can stay motivated and make consistent progress.

Dealing with frustration and setbacks

One of the biggest challenges of learning a new language is dealing with the frustration that comes with not understanding everything right away. It's important to remember that language learning is a process, and it takes time and practice to get better. Celebrate small successes, and don't be too hard on yourself when you make mistakes.

How to stay motivated and make consistent progress

To stay motivated, set achievable goals and track your progress. Use resources such as language learning apps, podcasts, or online courses to supplement your studies. You could also try finding a language learning partner or joining a language exchange group to practice speaking with other learners.

CONCLUSION: EMBRACING STRUCTURED AND ACCESSIBLE LANGUAGE LEARNING FOR PERSONAL AND PROFESSIONAL GROWTH

Learning a new language is a valuable investment in both personal and professional growth. Structured and accessible language learning can help you overcome the challenges of learning a new language, and provide you with a range of cognitive and professional benefits.

The continued importance of language learning in the global market

As the world becomes increasingly interconnected, the ability to communicate in multiple languages is becoming more important. Being able to speak another language can help you bridge cultural divides and connect with people from different backgrounds, making it an essential skill in today's global market.

The power of language to connect with others and broaden horizons

Beyond the cognitive and professional benefits, learning a new language can also broaden your horizons and help you connect with others. Language is a powerful tool for breaking down barriers and fostering understanding between people from different cultures. Whether you're traveling abroad, working with international clients, or simply trying to expand your social circle, learning a new language can enrich your life in countless ways. In conclusion, learning a new programming language is a valuable skill that can enhance your cognitive abilities, professional opportunities, and personal growth. By approaching language learning in a structured and accessible manner, you can overcome common challenges and make consistent progress toward your goals. Whether you are pursuing a career in programming or simply looking to expand your knowledge, embracing language learning is a powerful way to connect with others and broaden your horizons.

FAQ

What is the best programming language for beginners?

The best programming language for beginners will depend on their goals and interests. Some popular choices include Python, Java, and JavaScript. These languages have relatively simple syntax and are widely used in various industries.

How can I stay motivated while learning a new language?

Staying motivated while learning a new language can be challenging, especially when you encounter setbacks or difficulties. One effective strategy is to set achievable goals and celebrate your progress along the way. You can also find a language learning community or a study partner to keep you accountable and provide support.

What are the benefits of learning multiple programming languages?

Learning multiple programming languages can enhance your cognitive abilities and improve your problem-solving skills. It can also broaden your career opportunities and make you more versatile as a programmer.

Additionally, learning new languages can be a fun and rewarding way to expand your knowledge and challenge yourself.

How can I choose the right programming language for my project?

Choosing the right programming language for your project will depend on various factors, such as the project's scope, requirements, and target audience. You should consider the language's syntax, features, and compatibility with other technologies. It can also be helpful to seek advice from experts in the field or consult online resources.

Hands-on exercises and coding examples to reinforce learning.

Hands-on learning is a powerful approach to mastering new skills and concepts that is becoming increasingly popular in today's education and training landscape. By providing learners with opportunities to actively engage in the learning process through hands-on exercises and coding examples, they can develop a deeper understanding of the subject matter and improve their retention and recall of information. In this article, we will explore the benefits of hands-on learning, essential tools and resources for hands-on learning, and best practices for creating effective coding examples. Additionally, we will discuss common challenges and solutions in hands-on learning and explore ways to measure success in this approach.

INTRODUCTION TO HANDS-ON LEARNING

Learning through hands-on experiences has been a popular and effective teaching methodology for decades. It allows individuals to learn by actively engaging in a task or project instead of just passively taking in information. Hands-on learning encourages critical thinking, problem-solving, and collaboration, making it an ideal teaching method for coding and technical education.

Defining Hands-On Learning

Hands-on learning is a teaching methodology that encourages active participation and engagement. It involves practical activities and tasks that allow learners to gain skills, knowledge, and understanding through experimentation and exploration. It is a stimulus for learners to become more involved in their education and helps to create a deeper understanding of the material.

The Importance of Hands-On Learning

Hands-on learning is crucial for technical education, as it reinforces the practical skills needed to succeed in a real-world context. By doing so, students gain confidence and competence in their abilities. This approach to learning can also increase motivation, provide students with a deeper understanding of classroom material, and enhance their retention of the subject matter.

BENEFITS OF HANDS-ON EXERCISES AND CODING EXAMPLES

The use of hands-on exercises and coding examples in technical education has a multitude of benefits, including:

Active Learning

Hands-on exercises offer an active learning experience that creates a more engaging environment for students. Active learning encourages students to develop their problem-solving and critical thinking skills by applying concepts and theories in real-world contexts.

Retention and Recall

Hands-on learning approaches that include coding examples and exercises have been shown to improve learning retention and recall. When learners work on practical tasks, they are more likely to remember and apply the concepts they have learned in the future.

Increased Engagement

Hands-on exercises and coding examples are generally more interesting and engaging than passive, lecture-based instruction. Students are often more motivated and invested in the material when they can see its practical applications.

ESSENTIAL TOOLS AND RESOURCES FOR HANDS-ON LEARNING

Several tools and resources can facilitate effective hands-on learning in technical education.

Software Tools

Coding software, such as Visual Studio Code, Eclipse, or PyCharm, can be used to simulate real-world coding and software development activities. These tools can help learners identify and resolve coding errors, build applications, and test their software.

Hardware Tools

Hardware tools, like Raspberry Pi or Arduino boards, can be used to reinforce concepts and give learners practical experience in hardware design and development. These tools can be used in a variety of projects, from building robots to creating smart home gadgets.

Online Resources

There are many free resources available online that can aid in hands-on learning, such as coding tutorials, forums, and coding communities. These resources are incredibly helpful for learners looking to expand their knowledge base and skills.

HANDS-ON EXERCISES TO ENHANCE CODING SKILLS

There are various types of hands-on exercises and coding examples that you can utilize to improve your coding skills.

Coding Challenges

Coding challenges are tasks that require learners to solve complex coding problems within a set timeframe. These challenges can help learners develop their coding expertise by forcing them to think critically and creatively.

Mini Projects

Mini projects are small projects that focus on building a piece of software or hardware. These projects give learners experience in designing, coding and testing their software, which can improve their knowledge in a practical sense.

Collaborative Exercises

Collaborative exercises are group projects that encourage students to work together and share their expertise. These projects can help students learn valuable skills such as communication, teamwork, and project management.

BEST PRACTICES FOR CREATING EFFECTIVE CODING EXAMPLES

Hands-on exercises and coding examples are essential aspects of learning programming languages. They help in reinforcing the concepts taught and provide practical experience to apply them. Here are some best practices that you can follow to create effective coding examples:

Identifying the Learning Objective

Before creating the coding examples, it is crucial to identify the learning objectives. It helps in creating relevant and targeted examples. Define what you want the learners to achieve and structure the exercise accordingly.

Clear Instructions

Clear and concise instructions help the learners understand the task and what is expected of them. Elaborate on the expected outcome, and provide examples if needed. Ensure that the instructions are easy to follow and understand.

Gradual Complexity

Start with simple coding examples and gradually increase their complexity as the learners progress. Start with basic syntax and gradually move to more complex concepts. This approach helps the learners to build confidence and prevents overwhelming them.

COMMON CHALLENGES AND SOLUTIONS IN HANDS-ON LEARNING

While hands-on learning is an effective way to reinforce learning, it can come with its own set of challenges. Here are some common challenges and solutions:

Time Constraints

In a fast-paced learning environment, learners may feel that they do not have enough time to complete the exercises. To address this issue, create bite-sized exercises that can be completed in short intervals. Allocate time for practice and ensure that it is integrated into the learning schedule.

Lack of Motivation

Learners may lose motivation if the exercises are too difficult or do not have any real-life relevance. To keep learners motivated, create examples that are relevant to the learners' backgrounds and interests. Set achievable goals and provide regular feedback and encouragement to keep learners engaged.

Technical Issues

Technical issues such as software incompatibility and hardware failure can hinder hands-on learning. To address this issue, ensure that the learners have access to the required software and hardware. Offer technical support and troubleshooting tips to help learners overcome any technical obstacles.

MEASURING SUCCESS IN HANDS-ON LEARNING

Assessing the effectiveness of the hands-on learning approach is crucial to measure the learners' progress. Here are some assessment techniques and feedback methods:

Assessment Techniques

Use quizzes, exams, and coding challenges to assess the learners' understanding. Ask learners to complete exercises that demonstrate their understanding of the concepts taught. Provide feedback and explain how they can improve.

Feedback and Reflection

Provide regular feedback and encourage learners to reflect on what they have learned. Allow them to ask questions and seek clarification on any misunderstandings. Encourage learners to share their successes and challenges, and guide how they can improve.

CONCLUSION AND FUTURE DIRECTIONS

Hands-on learning is an effective way to reinforce learning in programming languages. Following the best practices mentioned above can help create effective coding examples that aid in the learning process. However, it is essential to address the challenges that learners face and use appropriate assessment techniques to measure success. The future of hands-on learning looks promising with the advent of new technologies such as virtual reality and augmented reality that can enhance the learning experience. In conclusion, hands-on exercises and coding examples are effective ways to reinforce learning and improve skills. By implementing the best practices discussed in this article and using the appropriate tools and resources, learners can enhance their engagement and retention of new material. As hands-on learning becomes more widespread, it will continue to be an important approach for educators and trainers to help learners achieve their full potential.

FAQ

What are the benefits of hands-on learning?

Hands-on learning provides several benefits, including increased engagement, active learning, and improved retention and recall. By allowing learners to actively engage in the learning process and apply new concepts and skills in practical exercises, hands-on learning can help them develop a deeper understanding of the material.

What tools and resources are necessary for hands-on learning?

Essential tools and resources for hands-on learning include hardware and software tools, as well as online resources such as tutorials and coding challenges. Depending on the subject matter, additional resources may be required to ensure learners have access to the necessary tools and equipment.

What are the best practices for creating effective coding examples?

Best practices for creating effective coding examples include identifying the learning objective, providing clear instructions, and gradually increasing the complexity of the exercise. Additionally, it's important to provide learners with feedback and opportunities for reflection to ensure they are achieving the desired learning outcomes.

How do you measure success in hands-on learning?

Success in hands-on learning can be measured through various assessment techniques, such as quizzes and practical exercises, as well as feedback and reflection from learners. Additionally, observing learners' behavior and engagement during the learning process can provide valuable insights into the effectiveness of hands-on learning.

Exploring different programming paradigms, including procedural, object-oriented, functional, and declarative.

Programming is an essential skill in today's digital age, and with the vast array of programming languages available, it can be difficult to determine which one to use for a particular project. However, choosing a programming language is not the only factor to consider when developing software. It is equally important to understand the programming paradigm that will be used. There are several programming paradigms available, including procedural, object-oriented, functional, and declarative. Each of these paradigms has its unique strengths and weaknesses, and understanding them can help developers to choose the right approach for their specific projects. In this article, we will explore the different programming paradigms, their key features, and their advantages and disadvantages.

1. Introduction to Programming Paradigms

What is a Programming Paradigm?

A programming paradigm is a way of approaching programming problems and designing solutions. It is a framework or style that guides developers on how to structure their code. Different paradigms have their own rules and guidelines that dictate how code should be organized and executed.

Why Understanding Programming Paradigms Matters

Understanding different programming paradigms is essential to becoming a skilled programmer. By learning different paradigms, developers can broaden their knowledge and skills, allowing them to tackle different programming problems and scenarios. Additionally, understanding the strengths and weaknesses of different paradigms can help developers choose the most appropriate one for a given programming task.

2. Procedural Programming

Definition of Procedural Programming

Procedural programming is a programming paradigm that involves breaking down a program into a set of procedures or functions that can be called one after another. Procedural programming follows a top-down approach, where each function is executed in the order defined in the program.

Key Concepts and Features of Procedural Programming

Key concepts of procedural programming include the use of subroutines and functions, the idea of modular programming, and the importance of sequencing in programming. Procedural programming accomplishes tasks using a series of well-defined steps, each of which is designed to perform a specific action.

Advantages and Disadvantages of Procedural Programming

The advantages of procedural programming include the ease of understanding and following the program flow since it follows a top-down approach. Additionally, procedural programming is efficient in performance and uses less memory since it only calls the required functions. However, it is less flexible than other programming paradigms and can lead to code duplication or redundancy.

2. Object-Oriented Programming

Definition of Object-Oriented Programming

Object-oriented programming is a programming paradigm that models the real world by representing everything as objects that have specific attributes and behaviors. It focuses on creating reusable code by organizing it into objects that interact with each other.

Key Concepts and Features of Object-Oriented Programming

Key concepts of object-oriented programming include encapsulation, inheritance, and polymorphism. Encapsulation is the idea of bundling data and behavior, inheritance is the ability for objects to inherit properties and behaviors from other objects, and polymorphism allows objects to take on different forms or behaviors.

Advantages and Disadvantages of Object-Oriented Programming

The advantages of object-oriented programming include its ability to create reusable code, enhance code maintainability and flexibility, and allow for better code organization. However, it can be complex to understand, and it might not be efficient in performance when dealing with large-scale applications.

2. Functional Programming

Definition of Functional Programming

Functional programming is a programming paradigm that involves programming using functions. It focuses on providing a clear set of instructions and data flows from input to output, without changing any external state or data.

Key Concepts and Features of Functional Programming

Key concepts of functional programming include the use of pure functions that have no side effects, immutability where data is never changed, higher-order functions that take in other functions as inputs, and recursion which allows functions to call themselves.

Advantages and Disadvantages of Functional Programming

The advantages of functional programming include its high level of modularity, easier debugging, and improved code readability. Functional programming is also well-suited for parallel processing. However, the paradigm can be challenging to understand, and it might not be ideal for all types of programming problems.

2. Declarative Programming

Definition of Declarative Programming

Declarative programming is a programming paradigm that focuses on describing the problem rather than describing how to solve the problem. In declarative programming, the programmer specifies a set of constraints or rules that the program must satisfy. The program then automatically generates a solution that satisfies those constraints.

Key Concepts and Features of Declarative Programming

One of the key features of declarative programming is that it separates the concerns of what the program is trying to accomplish from how the program should accomplish it. This separation allows for a clear and concise description of the problem without getting bogged down in implementation details.

Another important concept in declarative programming is the use of logic programming. Logic programming uses a set of predicates and rules to describe the problem space. The program then uses a backtracking algorithm to search for a solution that satisfies those predicates and rules.

Advantages and Disadvantages of Declarative Programming

One of the main advantages of declarative programming is that it can be easier to read and understand than other programming paradigms. By separating the concerns of what and how the program can focus on the problem at hand without getting bogged down in implementation details.

Another advantage of declarative programming is that it can be more concise and expressive than other programming paradigms. This makes it easier to write and maintain complex programs.

One disadvantage of declarative programming is that it can be less efficient than other programming paradigms. Since the program does not specify how the problem should be solved, the program must use more general algorithms that may not be as efficient as more specialized algorithms.

2. Comparison of Programming Paradigms

Side-by-Side Comparison of Paradigms

Here is a side-by-side comparison of the four main programming paradigms:

Procedural Programming:

-Focuses on step-by-step instructions that modify the state

-Uses functions and procedures to organize code

-Well-suited for low-level programming and performance-critical applications

Object-Oriented Programming:

-Focuses on organizing code into objects that encapsulate state and behavior

-Uses inheritance and polymorphism to reuse and extend code

-Well-suited for large-scale software development and complex applications

Functional Programming:

-Focuses on using pure functions that do not modify the state

-Uses higher-order functions and immutability to organize code

-Well-suited for concurrency and distributed systems

Declarative Programming:

-Focuses on describing the problem rather than how to solve it

-Uses logic programming and constraints to generate solutions

-Well-suited for complex problem domains and expert systems

Real-World Examples of Paradigms in Use

Procedural programming is commonly used in system programming, such as operating systems and device drivers. Object-oriented programming is commonly used in large-scale web applications, such as social networks and e-commerce sites. Functional programming is commonly used in financial applications and scientific computing. Declarative programming is commonly used in expert systems and artificial intelligence.

2. Choosing the Right Programming Paradigm

Factors to Consider When Selecting a Paradigm

When selecting a programming paradigm, there are several factors to consider. The first factor is the problem domain. Different problem domains may be better suited for different programming paradigms. For example, financial applications may be better suited for functional programming, while expert systems may be better suited for declarative programming.

Another factor to consider is the team's experience and expertise. If the team is already familiar with a particular programming paradigm, it may be easier and more efficient to use that paradigm.

Finally, performance requirements may also be a factor. Some programming paradigms, such as procedural programming, may be better suited for performance-critical applications.

Considerations for Specific Programming Tasks

For specific programming tasks, different programming paradigms may be better suited. For example, if the task involves data processing and analysis, functional programming may be a good choice. If the task involves building a user interface, object-oriented programming may be a good choice.

1. Future of Programming Paradigms

Emerging Trends in Programming Paradigms

One emerging trend in programming paradigms is the use of machine learning. Machine learning algorithms learn from data and can be used to automate programming tasks, such as bug fixing and code optimization.

Another emerging trend is the use of reactive programming. Reactive programming is a programming paradigm that involves building applications that respond to changes in their environment in real time.

What the Future Holds for Programming Paradigms

As technology continues to evolve, programming paradigms will continue to evolve as well. New programming paradigms will likely emerge to address the challenges of new technologies and problem domains. However, it is also likely that the four main programming paradigms will continue to be used for many years to come. In conclusion, understanding various programming paradigms is crucial in selecting the right approach for software development. Each paradigm has its unique features, strengths, and weaknesses. While some paradigms may be better suited for specific tasks, choosing the right paradigm ultimately depends on the developer's goals and objectives. By exploring the different programming paradigms, developers can broaden their programming knowledge and make informed decisions about their software development projects.

FAQS

What is a programming paradigm?

A programming paradigm is a way of classifying and organizing programming languages based on their underlying principles and concepts. It defines the way a program is designed and executed.

Which programming paradigm is the best?

There is no "best" programming paradigm. Each paradigm has its unique strengths and weaknesses and is better suited for specific programming tasks. The choice of programming paradigm depends on the specific project requirements and the developer's goals and objectives.

Can different programming paradigms be used together?

Yes, it is possible to use different programming paradigms together. This approach is known as a multi-paradigm programming language. Multi-paradigm programming languages can provide flexibility and allow developers to choose the right approach for a particular task.

How do I choose the right programming paradigm?

Choosing the right programming paradigm depends on several factors, including the project requirements, the available programming languages, the development team's expertise, and the budget. Before choosing a programming paradigm, it is essential to research and understands the different paradigms' key features and advantages and disadvantages.

Programming languages are the backbone of software development, and with so many programming languages available, it can be challenging to decide which one to use for a particular project. The language you choose can have far-reaching effects on your coding style and problem-solving approaches. Understanding language design choices is crucial in programming, as it allows you to choose the right language that matches your coding style and needs. In this article, we will explore how language design choices impact coding styles and problem-solving approaches. We will delve into the syntax, semantics, and features of object-oriented programming and functional programming and discuss how to choose the right language.

INTRODUCTION: LANGUAGE DESIGN CHOICES AND THEIR IMPACT ON CODING STYLES

Have you ever wondered why coding in one language feels completely different than coding in another language? Language design choices play a huge role in determining the coding style of programmers. These choices can affect everything from how developers approach solving problems to the way they write code.

What Are Language Design Choices?

Language design choices refer to the way a programming language is constructed. This includes things like syntax, which is the set of rules that govern how code is written, and semantics, which is the meaning behind the code. Other design choices include the programming paradigms a language supports, such as object-oriented or functional programming.

Why Do They Matter for Coding Styles and Problem-Solving Approaches?

Language design choices can greatly influence how developers approach problem-solving and what coding style they adopt. For instance, a language with strict syntax rules may encourage developers to write cleaner and more organized code. On the other hand, a language with loose syntax rules may encourage more creative solutions to problems.

Understanding how language design choices impact coding styles and problem-solving approaches is crucial for any programmer looking to improve their skills and become more versatile.

SYNTAX AND SEMANTICS: HOW THEY INFLUENCE PROBLEM-SOLVING APPROACHES

Understanding Syntax and Semantics

Syntax and semantics are two important language design choices that greatly affect how programmers write code and solve problems. Syntax refers to the set of rules that govern how code is written, while semantics refers to the meaning behind the code.

How Syntax and Semantics Impact Problem-Solving Approaches

The syntax and semantics of a programming language can greatly influence how developers approach problem-solving. For example, a language with strict syntax may encourage developers to write cleaner and more organized code, which can make it easier to solve problems. However, a language with complex syntax may require more effort to write code, which can make it more difficult to solve problems quickly.

Similarly, the semantics of a programming language can affect how developers approach problem-solving. A language with built-in functions and libraries may make solving certain problems easier, while a language with more abstract semantics may require developers to build their solutions from scratch.

OBJECT-ORIENTED PROGRAMMING: A LANGUAGE DESIGN CHOICE WITH FAR-REACHING EFFECTS

What Is Object-Oriented Programming?

Object-oriented programming is a programming paradigm based on the concept of objects, which are data structures that contain data and methods. These objects can interact with each other to solve problems and create more complex programs.

Features of Object-Oriented Programming

Some key features of object-oriented programming include encapsulation, inheritance, and polymorphism. Encapsulation refers to the ability to hide the implementation details of an object, while inheritance allows developers to create new objects based on existing ones. Polymorphism refers to the ability of objects to take on different forms, depending on their context.

How Object-Oriented Programming Impacts Coding Styles and Problem-Solving Approaches

Object-oriented programming can greatly impact coding styles and problem-solving approaches. For instance, it encourages developers to think about problems in terms of objects and how they interact with each other. This can lead to more modular and organized code, which can make it easier to solve complex problems.

However, object-oriented programming does require a certain level of understanding and skill, which can make it more difficult for beginners to adopt. Additionally, it may not be the best choice for all types of problems and projects.

Functional Programming: A Language Design Choice with Unique Problem-Solving Approaches

What Is Functional Programming?

Functional programming is a programming paradigm based on the concept of functions, which are data structures that take inputs and produce outputs. These functions can be combined to create solutions to complex problems.

Features of Functional Programming

Some key features of functional programming include immutability, higher-order functions, and declarative programming. Immutability refers to the idea that data structures should not be modified once they are created, while higher-order functions allow functions to be passed as arguments to other functions. Declarative programming refers to the idea that programs should be written in terms of what they do, rather than how they do it.

How Functional Programming Impacts Coding Styles and Problem-Solving Approaches

Functional programming can greatly impact coding styles and problem-solving approaches. For instance, it encourages developers to think about problems in terms of functions and how they can be combined to create solutions. This can lead to more concise and modular code, which can make it easier to solve complex problems.

However, functional programming requires a different way of thinking than more traditional imperative programming styles. It may also not be the best choice for all types of problems and projects.

Choosing the Right Language: Matching Design Choices to Your Coding Style and Needs

When starting a new software development project, choosing the right programming language is an important decision. The language you choose can have a profound impact on your coding style and problem-solving approaches. With so many languages to choose from, it's important to select one that aligns with your coding preferences and project needs.

Factors to Consider When Choosing a Programming Language

Before selecting a programming language, there are several factors to consider. One of the most important is the purpose of your project. Are you building a web application, mobile app, or desktop software? Each type of project may require different languages. Other important factors include the level of complexity of the project, the size of your development team, and the available resources, including libraries and IDEs.

Matching Language Design Choices to Your Coding Style and Needs

Each programming language has its own unique design choices, such as syntax and structure, that can impact your coding style and approach. For example, languages like Python have a focus on readability and simplicity, making them ideal for beginners or those who prefer a more straightforward coding style. On the other hand, languages like C++ are designed for performance and efficiency, making them ideal for complex projects that require high processing speed.

When choosing a language, it's important to consider how its design choices align with your coding style and needs. Do you prefer a language with strict typing and syntax, or one that allows for more flexibility and dynamic types? Do you prefer a language with a large community and extensive library support or one that allows for more customization and control over your code?

Conclusion: The Importance of Understanding Language Design Choices in Software Development

In conclusion, understanding the design choices of programming languages is crucial for software developers. By selecting a language that aligns with your coding style and project needs, you can improve your efficiency, productivity, and overall satisfaction with the development process.

Summary of Key Points

- Choosing the right programming language is important for software development.

- Factors to consider when choosing a language include project type, complexity, team size, and available resources.

- Language design choices impact coding style and problem-solving approaches.

- It's important to match language design choices to your coding style and needs.

Final Thoughts and Future Directions

As software development continues to evolve, so do programming languages and their design choices. Developers need to stay up-to-date with new languages and design paradigms to optimize their coding style and approach. Ultimately, choosing the right language can have a major impact on the success of your project, so it's worth taking the time to carefully consider your options. In conclusion, language design choices play a significant role in software development, affecting coding styles and problem-solving approaches. By understanding the syntax, semantics, and features of programming languages such as object-oriented and functional programming, developers can choose the right language that matches their coding style and needs. In today's fast-paced world of software development, it is essential to make informed decisions when selecting programming languages to ensure efficient and successful project outcomes.

FAQ

What are language design choices?

Language design choices are decisions made by the creators of a programming language regarding the syntax, semantics, and features of the language. These choices affect how the language is used, how problems are solved, and the coding style of the language.

How do language design choices impact coding styles and problem-solving approaches?

Language design choices can significantly impact coding styles and problem-solving approaches. For example, object-oriented programming languages are best suited for complex, large-scale projects that require a lot of collaboration, while functional programming languages are better suited for mathematical and scientific calculations.

How can I choose the right programming language for my project?

Choosing the right programming language for your project involves considering several factors, including the project's requirements, your team's coding style, and the language's design choices. It is essential to research and understand the syntax, semantics, and features of different programming languages to make an informed decision.

Can I use multiple programming languages in one project?

Yes, it is possible to use multiple programming languages in one project. This approach is often used when specific parts of the project require different programming languages. However, it is essential to ensure that the languages are compatible and can work together harmoniously.

Practical examples and case studies that demonstrate the power and versatility of each programming language.

Programming languages are ubiquitous in the world of software development, with each language offering its own unique set of features and advantages. From automating tasks in Python to building enterprise-level systems in Java to creating interactive web applications with JavaScript, there are countless practical examples and case studies that demonstrate the power and versatility of each language. In this article, we will explore some of the most popular programming languages and their applications in real-world scenarios. Whether you are a beginner or an experienced developer, this article will provide valuable insights into the world of programming languages and help you choose the right language for your next project.

INTRODUCTION: THE IMPORTANCE OF PROGRAMMING LANGUAGES

Programming languages are the building blocks of modern technology. They provide developers with a means to create software, websites, and applications that make our lives easier and more efficient. There are countless programming languages available today, each with its unique features and capabilities.

In this article, we'll explore some of the most popular programming languages and the practical applications of each. From automating tasks and building machine learning models with Python to creating interactive web applications with JavaScript, we'll demonstrate the power and versatility of these languages through real-world examples and case studies.

The Role of programming languages in modern software development

Programming languages are essential to modern software development, as they allow developers to create software that can automate tasks, analyze data, and communicate with other systems. They provide a way for computers to understand and interpret our instructions, allowing us to build complex systems that can accomplish a wide range of tasks.

As technology continues to evolve, programming languages will continue to play a crucial role in shaping our digital landscape. By mastering one or more programming languages, developers can create innovative solutions to complex problems and help drive the future of technology.

Choosing the right language for your project

Choosing the right programming language for your project is essential to its success. While some languages may be better suited for certain tasks than others, the choice ultimately depends on your specific needs and preferences.

When choosing a programming language, consider factors such as the size and complexity of your project, the availability of libraries and frameworks, and the experience and expertise of your development team. By carefully weighing these factors, you can choose the programming language that best meets your needs and helps you achieve your goals.

PYTHON: AUTOMATING TASKS AND MACHINE LEARNING

Python is a high-level, versatile programming language that is widely used for automating tasks, building data analysis tools, and creating machine learning models. Here are some practical examples of how Python can be used:

Introduction to Python and its features

Python is known for its readability and simplicity, making it a popular language for beginners and experienced developers alike. It has a wide range of built-in modules and libraries, making it easy to perform a variety of tasks without having to write a lot of code from scratch.

Automating tasks with Python

Python is frequently used for automating routine tasks, such as data entry, file management, and web scraping. By using Python scripts, developers can automate these tasks and save time and effort.

For example, a company may use Python to automatically extract data from online sources and save it to a database. This can help streamline business processes and improve efficiency.

Building machine learning models with Python

Python's simplicity and flexibility make it an ideal language for building machine-learning models. There are several popular libraries available, such as TensorFlow and Scikit-Learn, that can help developers build and train models quickly and easily.

For instance, a healthcare provider may use Python to build a machine-learning model that can predict patient outcomes based on their medical history. This can help improve the accuracy of diagnoses and treatment plans.

JAVA: BUILDING ENTERPRISE-LEVEL APPLICATIONS

Java is a popular programming language that is widely used for building enterprise-level applications. Here's how Java can be applied in practical settings:

Introduction to Java and its features

Java is known for its object-oriented programming capabilities and its ability to run on multiple platforms. This makes it a popular choice for building applications that can run on a wide range of devices and operating systems.

Building enterprise-level applications with Java

Java is commonly used for building enterprise-level applications, such as financial systems, customer relationship management tools, and inventory management systems. Its scalability and reliability make it a great choice for these types of applications.

For instance, a large corporation may use Java to build a custom CRM system that can manage customer information and transactions across multiple departments and locations.

Java vs other enterprise-level languages

While several programming languages can be used for building enterprise-level applications, Java is often preferred due to its robustness, security, and scalability. Other popular languages for enterprise development include C# and Ruby on Rails, each with its unique strengths and weaknesses.

JAVASCRIPT: CREATING INTERACTIVE WEB APPLICATIONS

JavaScript is a popular programming language that is widely used for creating interactive web applications. Here's how JavaScript can be applied in practical settings:

Introduction to JavaScript and its features

JavaScript is a client-side scripting language that is used to create dynamic and interactive web pages. It can be used to control web browsers, manipulate HTML and CSS, and add interactivity to web pages.

Creating interactive web applications with JavaScript

JavaScript is frequently used for creating interactive web applications, such as social media platforms, e-commerce sites, and online games. Its ability to interact with other technologies, such as APIs and databases, makes it a versatile tool for web development.

For example, a startup may use JavaScript to build a new social media platform that allows users to share and connect with others in real time. JavaScript can be used to create dynamic user interfaces, intelligent chatbots, and other interactive features that enhance the user experience.

Frameworks and libraries that use JavaScript

Several popular frameworks and libraries use JavaScript, such as React, Angular, and Node.js. These technologies provide developers with a powerful set of tools for creating complex and scalable web applications.

For instance, a streaming service may use Node.js to build a scalable and reliable video streaming platform. Node.js can be used to handle large amounts of data and traffic, ensuring a smooth and uninterrupted viewing experience for users.

C++: DESIGNING HIGH-PERFORMANCE SYSTEMS

C++ is a general-purpose programming language that is commonly used to create high-performance systems, such as operating systems, device drivers, video games, and high-frequency trading applications. Its features include low-level memory manipulation, object-oriented programming, and inline assembly code. C++ is known for its efficiency, speed, and control over system resources.

Introduction to C++ and its features

C++ was developed by Bjarne Stroustrup in 1983 as an extension of the C programming language. It adds features such as classes, templates, and exceptions to C, making it a more powerful and versatile language. C++ is often used in fields such as finance, aerospace, and gaming, where performance and control are crucial.

Designing high-performance systems with C++

C++ is valued for its ability to directly manipulate memory and hardware, allowing developers to create systems that are highly optimized and efficient. It is often used in embedded systems and real-time applications, where speed and reliability are critical. C++ is also a popular choice for creating high-frequency trading systems, which require extremely low latency and high throughput.

C++ vs other high-performance languages

C++ is not the only language used for high-performance systems. Other languages such as Rust, D, and Go have also gained popularity in recent years. Rust, for example, offers memory safety and thread safety features that make it a safer alternative to C++. D offers garbage collection and better memory management than C++. Go offers concurrency support and faster compile times than C++. However, C++ remains a popular choice for creating high-performance systems due to its long history, vast library support, and performance capabilities.

RUBY: RAPID PROTOTYPING AND WEB DEVELOPMENT

Ruby is a general-purpose programming language that is often used for web development, scripting, and rapid prototyping. Its features include dynamic typing, garbage collection, and metaprogramming. Ruby is known for its readability and ease of use.

Introduction to Ruby and its features

Ruby was created by Yukihiro "Matz" Matsumoto in 1995 as a scripting language that was more powerful and elegant than Perl and Python. Its syntax is designed to be easily readable and expressive. Ruby is often used with the Ruby on Rails web development framework, which provides a powerful set of tools for building web applications.

Rapid prototyping with Ruby

Ruby is often used for rapid prototyping due to its ease of use and ability to quickly create working prototypes. Its expressive syntax allows developers to write code that is concise and easy to understand. Ruby is also commonly used in the development of web applications, where it can help streamline development and improve productivity.

Web development with Ruby and its frameworks

Ruby on Rails is the most popular framework for web development with Ruby. It provides a set of conventions and tools that make it easy to create web applications quickly and efficiently. Rails provide features such as scaffolding, which generates boilerplate code for common tasks, and ActiveRecord, which simplifies database access. Other popular Ruby web frameworks include Sinatra and Hanami.

CASE STUDIES: REAL-WORLD EXAMPLES OF PROGRAMMING LANGUAGE APPLICATION

Case study 1: Python in data science at Netflix

Python is a popular language for data science and machine learning applications. Netflix uses Python extensively in its recommendation engine, which helps suggest content to users based on their viewing history. Python's data processing capabilities and extensive library support make it a valuable tool for data analysis and visualization.

Case study 2: Java in building enterprise-level systems at Amazon

Java is a versatile language that is used for a variety of applications, including enterprise-level systems. Amazon uses Java in its backend systems, including Amazon Web Services, which provides cloud computing infrastructure for businesses. Java's security features, scalability, and vast community support make it a popular choice for large-scale systems.

Case study 3: JavaScript in creating interactive web applications at Facebook

JavaScript is the primary language used for web development. Facebook uses it extensively in its front-end systems, including its React framework, which simplifies the process of building interactive user interfaces. JavaScript's ability to run natively in web browsers makes it a valuable tool for creating responsive and dynamic web applications.

Case study 4: C++ in designing high-performance systems at Google

C++ is a valuable tool for creating high-performance systems, and Google uses it extensively in its search engine and other systems. C++'s low-level memory manipulation and ability to directly access hardware make it a powerful tool for building highly optimized systems.

Case Study 5: Ruby in rapid prototyping at Airbnb

Ruby is often used for rapid prototyping, and Airbnb uses it extensively in its development process. Ruby's syntax and readability make it easy to quickly create working prototypes, and its ability to interact with other technologies, such as JavaScript, makes it a valuable tool for web development.

CONCLUSION: CHOOSING THE RIGHT LANGUAGE FOR YOUR PROJECT

Key takeaways from the article

Choosing the right programming language for a project depends on a variety of factors, including performance requirements, development time, available libraries and frameworks, and developer skills. Each language has its strengths and weaknesses and is best suited for specific tasks. C++, for example, is a powerful language for creating high-performance systems, while Ruby is often used for rapid prototyping and web development.

Factors to consider when choosing a programming language

When choosing a programming language for a project, it is important to consider factors such as the project's requirements, the size and experience of the development team, available libraries and frameworks, and the language's performance and scalability. It is also important to consider the language's ecosystem and community support, as these can play a crucial role in the success of a project. In conclusion, programming languages are essential tools for modern software development, and their versatility cannot be overstated. By understanding the unique features and applications of each language, developers can choose the best tool for their particular project, leading to more efficient and effective software development. We hope this article has provided valuable insights and inspired you to explore the possibilities of different programming languages.

FAQ

Which programming language is the best?

There is no single "best" programming language, as each language has its own unique advantages and use cases. The choice of language depends on the project requirements and the developer's familiarity with the language. It's important to choose the language that fits the project needs and the team's skill set.

What are the factors to consider when choosing a programming language?

Some of the key factors to consider when choosing a programming language include the project requirements, the team's skill set, the available resources, and the language's popularity and community support. It's important to choose a language that is well-suited for the task at hand and has a strong community and support system.

What are some popular applications of each programming language?

Python is often used in data science and machine learning applications, Java is popular in building enterprise-level systems, JavaScript is commonly used for web development, C++ is often used for high-performance systems, and Ruby is popular for rapid prototyping and web development. However, these are just a few examples, and each language has its own unique set of applications and use cases.

What are some resources for learning more about programming languages?

There are countless resources available for learning programming languages, including online tutorials, books, and courses. Some popular resources for learning programming languages include Codecademy, Udemy, Coursera, and edX. Additionally, there are many online communities and forums where developers can ask questions and share knowledge with others.

Building applications such as web development, mobile apps, data analysis, and automation.

In today's digital age, the demand for applications is at an all-time high. Companies of all sizes are striving to create interactive and engaging websites, mobile apps, and tools that automate their processes and extract valuable insights from data. Building applications requires a deep understanding of different technologies, programming languages, and development tools. In this article, we will explore the world of application development, including web development, mobile app development, data analysis, and automation. We'll discuss the importance of building high-quality applications, best practices for developing them, and emerging trends and innovations in the field.

INTRODUCTION TO BUILDING APPLICATIONS

Building applications is a critical aspect of modern-day technology. From web development to mobile apps, data analysis to automation, application development plays a fundamental role in shaping the digital world we live in today. In this article, we'll explore the different types of applications and their importance in the current technological landscape.

The Importance of Application Development

At its core, application development is the process of creating software programs that run on various platforms and devices. Applications provide solutions to real-life problems, automate repetitive tasks, and make our lives more comfortable and efficient. The ever-increasing demand for new and innovative applications makes it a highly rewarding and lucrative field.

Understanding the Different Types of Applications

There are several types of applications, each with a unique purpose and function. Web development, mobile apps, data analysis, and automation are among the most popular application development fields. Web development deals with creating interactive and dynamic websites, while mobile app development focuses on designing and developing customized mobile applications. Data analysis involves extracting insights and making data-driven decisions, and automation aims to streamline repetitive tasks.

WEB DEVELOPMENT: CREATING INTERACTIVE AND DYNAMIC WEBSITES

Overview of Web Development

Web development is a broad term that refers to the process of creating websites. It involves a range of skills, including coding, graphic design, user experience, and project management. Web developers use various front-end and back-end frameworks to create interactive and dynamic websites.

Front-End Web Development

Front-end web development deals with creating the visual and interactive aspects of a website that users see. It involves using languages such as HTML, CSS, and JavaScript to design the website's layout, font, colors, and visual elements.

Back-End Web Development

Back-end web development involves creating the server-side functionality of a website. It involves using languages such as PHP, Python, or Ruby to develop the back-end infrastructure of a website, such as a server, database, and API.

Full-Stack Web Development

Full-stack web development encompasses both front-end and back-end web development. A full-stack developer has the skills and knowledge to create a complete web application independently.

MOBILE APPS: DESIGNING AND DEVELOPING CUSTOMIZED MOBILE APPLICATIONS

The Mobile App Development Process

Mobile app development involves creating customized software applications that run on mobile devices such as smartphones and tablets. The mobile app development process includes planning, designing, developing, testing, and deploying the application.

Native App Development

Native app development involves building an application specifically for a particular platform, such as iOS or Android. Native app development provides better performance and access to the device's features.

Hybrid App Development

Hybrid app development involves building an application that can run on multiple platforms. Hybrid apps are developed using web technology such as HTML, CSS, and JavaScript and use a wrapper to run as a native app on the target platform.

DATA ANALYSIS: EXTRACTING INSIGHTS AND MAKING DATA-DRIVEN DECISIONS

Introduction to Data Analysis

Data analysis involves using statistical and computational methods to extract insights from data. The goal of data analysis is to understand patterns and relationships within data and make data-driven decisions.

Data Collection and Preparation

Data collection and preparation involve collecting relevant data and cleaning and organizing it in a format that can be analyzed. This step is crucial since the accuracy and completeness of the data impact the insights derived from data analysis.

Data Visualization

Data visualization involves presenting data in a graphical format that is easy to understand and interpret. Data visualization helps analysts communicate their findings effectively.

Statistical Analysis and Machine Learning

Statistical analysis and machine learning involve using mathematical models and algorithms to analyze data. Statistical analysis involves using descriptive and inferential statistics to identify patterns and relationships within data. Machine learning involves using algorithms to train models on data and make predictions or decisions based on new data.

AUTOMATION: STREAMLINING PROCESSES AND INCREASING EFFICIENCY

Automation has become an essential part of application development, making the process faster and more efficient than ever before. By using automation, developers can streamline complex processes and avoid manual errors.

Benefits of Automation

One of the primary benefits of automation is that it reduces the time and effort required to complete repetitive tasks. Instead of spending hours on manual processes, developers can use automation tools to do the work for them. Automation also improves the accuracy and consistency of tasks, reducing the chances of human errors.

Automating Business Processes

Automation is a powerful tool for businesses as it allows them to automate a variety of tasks, such as invoicing, data entry, and customer support. Automating these tasks frees up time for employees to focus on more important tasks, such as customer service and innovation.

Automating Testing and Deployment

Automation is also useful in testing and deploying applications. By automating testing, developers can quickly identify issues and fix them before the product is released. They can also automate the deployment process, ensuring that the product is deployed efficiently and reliably.

CHOOSING THE RIGHT DEVELOPMENT TOOLS AND TECHNOLOGIES

Choosing the right tools and technologies is crucial when it comes to application development. It can make a significant difference in the quality and performance of the final product.

Overview of Development Tools and Technologies

There are a variety of tools and technologies available for application development. Some of the most popular include programming languages like Python, JavaScript, and Java, as well as web development frameworks like React, Angular, and Vue.js.

Factors to Consider When Choosing Development Tools and Technologies

When choosing development tools and technologies, developers must consider several factors, such as the requirements of the project, the experience of the development team, and the scalability of the solution.

Popular Development Tools and Technologies

Some of the most popular development tools and technologies include Git for version control, Jenkins for continuous integration and deployment, and Docker for containerization.

BEST PRACTICES FOR BUILDING HIGH-QUALITY APPLICATIONS

High-quality applications are critical to success in today's digital world. To achieve this, developers should follow some best practices.

Code Quality and Maintainability

Writing clean, maintainable code is essential for building high-quality applications. Code that is easy to read and understand is more comfortable to maintain and update over time.

Testing and Debugging

Testing and debugging applications are vital to ensure the quality of the product. Developers should test the application thoroughly to identify and fix bugs and errors.

Security and Data Privacy

Security and data privacy are critical concerns for application development. Developers should ensure that their applications are secure and protect user data from potential attacks.

FUTURE TRENDS AND INNOVATIONS IN APPLICATION DEVELOPMENT

The field of application development is always evolving, and developers should keep up with the latest trends and innovations.

Emerging Technologies and Frameworks

Emerging technologies such as Blockchain, the Internet of Things (IoT), and augmented reality (AR) are transforming the way we build and interact with applications.

The Impact of Artificial Intelligence and Machine Learning

Artificial Intelligence (AI) and Machine Learning (ML) are revolutionizing the way applications are developed and deployed. These technologies enable applications to learn and adapt to user behavior and provide personalized experiences.

Advancements in User Experience Design

User experience (UX) design is an essential aspect of application development. Advancements in UX design techniques and tools are making it easier for developers to create user-friendly and intuitive applications. In conclusion, building applications is a complex process that requires diverse skill sets and in-depth knowledge of different technologies. By following best practices and staying up-to-date with the latest trends and innovations, developers can create high-quality applications that meet the needs of businesses and consumers alike. Whether you're interested in web development, mobile app development, data analysis, or automation, the world of application development is a fascinating and rewarding field to explore.

FREQUENTLY ASKED QUESTIONS

What programming languages are commonly used for web development?

Some popular programming languages for web development include HTML, CSS, JavaScript, PHP, Python, and Ruby.

What are some tools and technologies used for data analysis?

Tools for data analysis include programming languages like R and Python, data visualization tools like Tableau and D3.js, and machine learning platforms like TensorFlow and Scikit-Learn.

What are some benefits of automating business processes?

Automating business processes can save time and money, increase efficiency, reduce errors, and improve overall productivity.

What are some emerging trends in application development?

Emerging trends in application development include the use of artificial intelligence and machine learning, the rise of low-code development platforms, and the increasing importance of cybersecurity and data privacy.

A side-by-side comparison of programming languages, highlighting their strengths, weaknesses, and ideal use cases.

Programming languages are the backbone of modern technology and are used to create virtually every software, website, and application in existence today. Given the numerous programming languages available, choosing the right one can be a daunting task. Each language has its strengths and weaknesses, and it is important to select the one that fits your specific needs. In this article, we'll provide an in-depth comparison of different programming languages, including their strengths, weaknesses, and ideal use cases. Through this, we aim to help you identify the programming language that best suits your unique requirements and skillsets.

1. Introduction to Programming Languages

Programming languages are the backbone of the digital world. They are used to build software, websites, mobile apps, and operating systems. Choosing the right programming language is crucial because each language has its strengths and weaknesses. The wrong choice can result in slower development times, less efficient code, and a higher degree of frustration. In this article, we'll break down the strengths and weaknesses of popular programming languages and what factors you should consider when choosing one.

The Importance of Choosing the Right Programming Language

Choosing the right programming language is crucial because it affects the development process from start to finish. Different programming languages have varying levels of difficulty, syntax, and functionality. Choosing the wrong language can cause significant problems, such as limited functionality, slower development times, and difficulties scaling.

Factors to Consider When Choosing a Programming Language

When choosing a programming language, several factors should be taken into account, such as the project's scope, deadlines, the complexity of the project, and the available development team. Other factors to consider include the language's learning curve, availability of resources, and compatibility with other tools and technologies. By considering all these factors, you can identify the ideal programming language for your project.

3. Strengths and Weaknesses of Programming Languages

Each programming language has its own set of strengths and weaknesses. Understanding these pros and cons can help you determine if a particular language is suitable for your project.

Understanding the Pros and Cons of Different Programming Languages

Some programming languages are better suited for specific tasks than others. For example, Python is excellent for data science and machine learning, while Java is better for enterprise applications. Understanding the pros and cons of each language can help you select the right tool for the job.

Factors that Affect the Strengths and Weaknesses of Programming Languages

Several factors can affect a programming language's strengths and weaknesses, such as the level of experience of the development team, the project's requirements, and the target audience's needs. The language's compatibility with other tools and technologies can also play a role in its strengths and weaknesses.

3. Ideal Use Cases for Popular Programming Languages

There are many popular programming languages in use today, each with its strengths and weaknesses. Understanding the ideal use cases for each language can help you determine the best tool for your project.

Overview of the Top Programming Languages in Use Today

Some of the top programming languages in use today include Python, Java, C++, C#, JavaScript, and Ruby. Each of these languages has a specific set of use cases, depending on the target audience and project requirements.

Ideal Use Cases for Popular Programming Languages, such as:

3.
4. Python: Ideal for data science, artificial intelligence, and web development.
5.
6. Java: Ideal for enterprise applications and Android app development.
7.
8. C++: Ideal for video game development, high-performance applications, and hardware-level programming.

9.

10.   C#: Ideal for Windows desktop applications, enterprise software, and gaming.

11.

12.   JavaScript: Ideal for web development, web applications, front-end, and back-end development.

13.

14.   Ruby: Ideal for web development, building dynamic websites, and developing web applications.

15.

3. Comparing Popular Programming Languages

Comparing popular programming languages is essential to identify the right choice for your project.

Overview of the Comparison Process

The comparison process involves analyzing the strengths and weaknesses of each language based on specific factors.

Factors Used to Compare Programming Languages

The factors used to compare programming languages include cost, performance, syntax, community support, popularity, and compatibility. By comparing languages using these factors, you can determine the most suitable language for your project.2>7. C++ vs C#: Which is the Best Choice for Game Development?

Overview of C++ and C#

Features and Characteristics of C++ and C#

Comparison of C++ and C# in terms of:

3.
4. Performance and Efficiency
5.
6. Availability of Game Engines and Libraries
7.
8. Community and Industry Support
9.
   10. Development Tools and Resources
   11.
   12. Other Factors
   13.

3. PHP vs Python: Which is Better for Web Development?

Overview of PHP and Python

Features and Characteristics of PHP and Python

Comparison of PHP and Python in terms of:

1. Java vs Python: A Side-by-Side Comparison

Overview of Java and Python

Java and Python are two of the most popular programming languages in the world. Java was created by James Gosling at Sun Microsystems in 1995 and has since then been used for developing web and mobile applications, enterprise systems, and games. Python, on the other hand, was created by Guido van Rossum in 1989 and is widely used for web development, scientific computing, data analysis, and artificial intelligence.

Features and Characteristics of Java and Python

Java is an object-oriented programming language that is known for its platform independence, static type system, and robust security features. It is designed to be scalable, maintainable, and portable, making it an ideal choice for larger-scale applications where performance and reliability are crucial.

Python, on the other hand, is a dynamically-typed, interpreted language that is known for its simplicity, ease of use, and rapid development capabilities. It has a large standard library and is an ideal choice for projects that require quick prototyping or data analysis.

Comparison of Java and Python in terms of:

Syntax and Readability:

Python has a simple and readable syntax that makes it easier for beginners to learn and write code. Java, on the other hand, has a more complex and verbose syntax that can be intimidating for new programmers.

Performance and Execution Speed:

Java is known for its high-performance capabilities and is often used for developing systems that require fast processing speeds. Python, on the other hand, is slower than Java due to its interpreted nature but offers a more efficient development process.

Community Support and Resources:

Both Java and Python have large and active communities that provide support, resources, and libraries for their respective languages.

Industry Applications and Trends:

Java is widely used in enterprise systems, web and mobile applications, and game development. Python is often used for scientific computing, data analysis, machine learning, and web development.

Other Factors:

Java is known for its robust security features, while Python is known for its ease of use and quick development capabilities.

1. JavaScript vs Ruby: Which is Better for Web Development?

Overview of JavaScript and Ruby

JavaScript has been around since the early days of the web and is widely used for front-end web development. Ruby, on the other hand, is a newer language that was created in the mid-1990s and is known for its simplicity, readability, and ease of use.

Features and Characteristics of JavaScript and Ruby

JavaScript is a dynamically-typed, interpreted language that is used for creating interactive and dynamic web pages. It is often used in conjunction with HTML and CSS to create front-end user interfaces.

Ruby, on the other hand, is a dynamic, object-oriented language that is known for its simplicity and readability. It is often used for developing web applications, automation scripts, and backend systems.

Comparison of JavaScript and Ruby in terms of:

Usability and Ease of Learning:

JavaScript has a steeper learning curve due to its complex syntax and concepts. However, it is widely used and has a wealth of resources available for learning and development. Ruby, on the other hand, has a simpler syntax and is easier to learn.

Performance and Scalability:

JavaScript is known for its speed and performance and is often used for creating complex web applications. Ruby, on the other hand, is slower than JavaScript and is often used for developing smaller-scale web applications.

Integration with Web Development Frameworks:

Both JavaScript and Ruby have a wealth of frameworks available for web development, such as React, Angular, and Ruby on Rails. However,

JavaScript frameworks tend to be more popular and widely used.

Libraries and Plugins:

JavaScript has a massive library of plugins and libraries available, making it easier to develop complex web applications. Ruby, on the other hand, has a smaller library but still has a variety of useful libraries available.

Other Factors:

JavaScript is widely used for front-end web development, while Ruby is often used for back-end development. JavaScript also has a larger community and is more commonly used in the industry.

1. C++ vs C#: Which is the Best Choice for Game Development?

Overview of C++ and C#

C++ is a high-performance, low-level language that is commonly used for developing games. C#, on the other hand, is a newer language that was created by Microsoft and is widely used for developing Windows applications, including games.

Features and Characteristics of C++ and C#

C++ is a complex, statically-typed language that is known for its performance and low-level control over hardware. It is often used for creating resource-intensive games that require high-speed processing and low-level hardware control.

C#, on the other hand, is a simpler, dynamically-typed language that is often used for developing games on the Windows platform. It is known for its ease of use, simplicity, and faster development time.

Comparison of C++ and C# in terms of:

Performance and Efficiency:

C++ is known for its high performance and is often used for developing resource-intensive games. C#, on the other hand, is slower but offers faster development time and better memory management.

Availability of Game Engines and Libraries:

Both C++ and C# have a variety of game engines and libraries available, such as Unreal Engine and Unity. However, C++ is known to have more high-performance engines and libraries available.

Community and Industry Support:

C++ hasIn conclusion, choosing the right programming language requires careful consideration of multiple factors, including the project requirements and your own experience and expertise. By comparing and contrasting the most popular programming languages, we hope that you are better equipped to choose the right tool for your next project. Remember, learning a new language takes time and effort, but the rewards can be immense when it comes to building efficient and effective software.

FAQS

How do I know which programming language is right for me?

Identifying the right programming language depends on various factors, such as the nature and scope of your project, your familiarity with programming, and your future career goals. You should evaluate each programming language's strengths and weaknesses to determine which one aligns with your objectives.

What are some common programming languages used today?

Some of the most used programming languages today include Python, Java, C++, JavaScript, Ruby, PHP, and Swift. These languages have different strengths and weaknesses, making them ideal for different types of applications.

Why is it essential to choose the right programming language?

Choosing the right programming language can help you optimize your development process and create more efficient, effective, and scalable applications. Moreover, selecting the right programming language can streamline your project's development process, save you time and money, and increase your overall success rate.

What are some resources available for learning programming languages?

There are numerous resources available for learning programming languages, including online courses, forums, tutorial videos, and interactive coding platforms like Codecademy, Udemy, and Coursera. Additionally, many programming languages have vast online communities where developers can ask questions, share ideas, and access helpful resources.

Helping readers make informed decisions when choosing the right language for a specific project.

Choosing the right programming language for your project is a critical decision that can have a significant impact on the success of your development efforts. With so many programming languages available, it can be challenging to determine which one is best suited for your project. In this article, we will explore the critical factors to consider when choosing a programming language, popular programming languages, and their applications, and how to evaluate the pros and cons of different programming languages. We will also provide tips for making informed decisions about language selection, best practices for working with multiple languages in a project and staying up-to-date with the latest language trends and developments. By the end of this article, you will have a solid understanding of how to choose the right programming language for your project and make informed decisions that will help ensure its success.

UNDERSTANDING THE IMPORTANCE OF CHOOSING THE RIGHT LANGUAGE

Why Language Selection Matters for Project Success

Choosing the right programming language is crucial for the success of any project. The programming language you choose has a direct impact on many aspects of your project, including development time, scalability, security, and maintenance. A poor choice of programming language can lead to problems down the line, such as difficulty finding experienced developers or the inability to meet project requirements.

The Consequences of Choosing the Wrong Programming Language

Choosing the wrong programming language can have serious consequences. It can result in a project that is more expensive, more difficult to maintain, less scalable, and less secure. It can also lead to slower development times and a reduced ability to meet project requirements. In addition, choosing the wrong programming language can make it difficult to find experienced developers.

FACTORS TO CONSIDER WHEN CHOOSING A PROGRAMMING LANGUAGE

Project Requirements and Constraints

The programming language you choose should be based on the specific requirements and constraints of your project. Consider factors such as the size and complexity of your project, the available hardware and software resources, and any specific performance requirements. Additionally, consider any budget and timeline constraints that may impact the choice of programming language.

Technical Skills and Experience of the Development Team

The technical skills and experience of your development team should also be considered when choosing a programming language. If your team is experienced in a particular language, it may be more efficient to use that language for your project. On the other hand, if your team has little experience in a particular language, it may be more difficult and time-consuming to complete the project using that language.

Costs and Timeframes

Costs and timeframes are important considerations when choosing a programming language. Some programming languages are more expensive to use than others, and some may take longer to develop. Additionally, some languages may require more training or support, which can increase costs and extend timelines.

POPULAR PROGRAMMING LANGUAGES AND THEIR APPLICATIONS

Introduction to Popular Programming Languages

There are many programming languages to choose from, each with its strengths and weaknesses. Some of the most popular programming languages include Java, Python, C++, and JavaScript.

Applications and Use Cases for Each Programming Language

Each programming language has its strengths and applications. For example, Java is commonly used for enterprise applications, while Python is often used for scientific computing and data analysis. C++ is popular for system programming and game development, while JavaScript is primarily used for web development.

EVALUATING PROS AND CONS OF DIFFERENT PROGRAMMING LANGUAGES

Pros and Cons of Popular Programming Languages (e.g. Java, Python, C++)

Each programming language has its pros and cons. For example, Java is known for its scalability and portability but can be slower than other languages. Python is easy to learn and has a large user community, but can be slower for certain tasks. C++ is fast and efficient but can be more difficult to learn and has a steeper learning curve.

Factors to Help You Evaluate Different Programming Languages

When evaluating different programming languages, consider factors such as ease of use, performance, scalability, and community support. Additionally, consider factors such as the availability of experienced developers, the cost and availability of tools and resources, and any specific requirements or constraints of your project.

TIPS FOR MAKING INFORMED DECISIONS ABOUT LANGUAGE SELECTION

Choosing the right programming language for a project can be a daunting task, but there are key factors to consider that will help you make an informed decision.

Best Practices for Evaluating Programming Languages

Before selecting a programming language, it's important to assess your project's requirements and your development team's skill sets. Research the various programming languages and review their documentation and user communities. Consider the language's popularity, stability, scalability, and performance. Additionally, it's important to evaluate the available tools and frameworks that support the language.

How to Avoid Common Pitfalls When Choosing a Programming Language

One common mistake when selecting a programming language is choosing based solely on familiarity or popularity. It's important to prioritize the best language for your project's needs rather than the most popular. Ensure that the language you choose is well-suited to your project's requirements and that your team has the necessary expertise to work with it.

BEST PRACTICES FOR WORKING WITH MULTIPLE LANGUAGES IN A PROJECT

While using multiple programming languages in a single project can be challenging, it can also provide benefits such as improved performance and flexibility.

Challenges and Benefits of Working with Multiple Languages

Working with multiple programming languages can introduce challenges such as integration issues and additional complexity but can also allow for the use of specialized tools and libraries. It may also allow for more efficient use of available resources, such as utilizing one language for back-end processing and another for front-end development.

How to Manage Multiple Languages Effectively

To manage multiple languages effectively, establish clear communication and collaboration channels within your development team. Maintain documentation of the languages and their individual use cases. It's also important to ensure that the different languages work well together and integrate seamlessly.

STAYING UP-TO-DATE WITH THE LATEST LANGUAGE TRENDS AND DEVELOPMENTS

Staying current with the latest language trends and developments is essential to ensure that your projects stay relevant, efficient, and effective.

Why It's Important to Stay Current with Language Trends

Programming languages and development trends are constantly evolving. Staying current allows you to leverage emerging technologies and maintain a competitive edge in the industry. It also helps to stay ahead of potential security vulnerabilities and bug fixes.

Tips for Staying Informed of New Language Developments

Stay engaged with the development community by attending conferences, participating in online forums, and following industry thought leaders. Keep an eye on industry publications and blogs, and sign up for newsletters that focus on language updates and trends. Following the development community on Twitter or LinkedIn is another way to stay informed about the latest trends and updates. In conclusion, choosing the right programming language for your project is a crucial decision that requires careful consideration of various factors. By following the best practices and tips outlined in this article, you can make informed decisions about language selection and increase your chances of project success. Remember to always stay up-to-date with the latest language trends and developments, and don't be afraid to ask for help from experts in the field. With the right approach, you can choose the programming language that best suits your project's needs and achieve your development goals.

FAQ

What are the critical factors to consider when choosing a programming language?

When choosing a programming language, some critical factors to consider include project requirements and constraints, technical skills and experience of the development team, and costs and timeframes. Other considerations may include the language's performance, portability, and scalability.

How do I evaluate the pros and cons of different programming languages?

To evaluate the pros and cons of different programming languages, you can consider factors such as the language's popularity and community support, its performance, scalability, and maintainability. You can also compare the language's syntax and structure to see which one is best suited for your project's requirements.

What are the best practices for working with multiple languages in a project?

When working with multiple languages in a project, it's essential to set clear guidelines and standards for development and establish effective communication channels between team members. You may also want to ensure that the development environment is configured correctly to support multiple languages and use tools that can help manage the integration between different languages.

How can I stay up-to-date with the latest language trends and developments?

To stay up-to-date with the latest language trends and developments, it's essential to participate in online communities, attend conferences and workshops, and read industry publications and blogs. You can also follow industry leaders and influencers on social media platforms to stay informed about the latest trends and developments.

Exploring emerging languages and trends in the programming landscape, such as machine learning, blockchain, and the Internet of Things (IoT).

The programming landscape is constantly evolving, and keeping up with emerging languages and trends has become more important than ever. From machine learning to blockchain and the Internet of Things (IoT), programming has gone beyond just coding applications and websites. It now involves building complex systems, analyzing large amounts of data, and developing secure and reliable solutions. In this article, we will explore the latest trends in programming and provide an overview of emerging languages like Rust and Swift. We will also delve into game-changing technologies like machine learning, blockchain, and IoT, and discuss their potential impact on the tech industry. So, let's dive into the evolving world of programming and discover what the future holds.

1. Introduction: The Evolution of Programming Landscape

The world of programming has come a long way since the 1940s when the first electronic computer was developed. The evolution of programming languages and trends has been fascinating, with new technologies and languages emerging every day. Programming has become an integral part of our daily lives, touching everything from smartphones to medical devices and industrial systems.

Programming Landscape: A Brief History of Programming Languages and Trends

Over the years, programming has seen a shift from low-level languages such as assembly language to high-level languages like Python and Ruby. The rise of the internet led to the emergence of web development languages like HTML, CSS, and JavaScript. With the proliferation of handheld devices, mobile apps development languages like Swift and Kotlin became popular.

In recent years, there has been a surge in new programming languages and trends, such as machine learning, blockchain, and the Internet of Things (IoT). These emerging technologies have captured the attention of programmers and businesses alike and are expected to shape the future of programming.

4. Emerging Languages: An Overview of Latest Trends in Programming

In this section, we will explore some of the latest trends in programming languages.

Rust: A New Safe and Fast Systems Programming Language

Rust is a safe and fast systems programming language that has been gaining popularity in recent years. It was developed by Mozilla and is designed to be efficient and secure. Rust is perfect for systems programming, where performance, safety, and security are critical.

WebAssembly: The Future of Web Development

WebAssembly is a new binary format for web applications that promises to bring native-like performance to the browser. It is designed to be a low-level assembly language for the web and is already being used by major tech companies like Google, Microsoft, and Mozilla.

Swift: The Preferred Language for iOS Development

Swift is a general-purpose, multi-paradigm programming language developed by Apple for iOS, macOS, watchOS, and tvOS development. It is designed to be safe, fast, and interactive and has quickly become the preferred language for iOS development.

4. Machine Learning: A Game-Changing Approach to Programming

In recent years, machine learning has emerged as a game-changing approach to programming.

Introduction to Machine Learning: Basics and Concepts

Machine learning is a subset of artificial intelligence that involves training algorithms to make predictions from data. It is used in a wide range of applications, from image recognition and speech recognition to fraud detection and stock prediction.

Python is the Preferred Language for Machine Learning

Python has emerged as the preferred language for machine learning due to its simplicity, ease of use, and the vast library of machine learning frameworks. Python libraries like TensorFlow, Keras, and PyTorch have made it easier for developers to build and deploy machine learning models.

Applications of Machine Learning in Various Industries

Machine learning is being used in various industries, including healthcare, finance, and manufacturing. In healthcare, machine learning is being used for disease diagnosis and drug discovery. In finance, machine learning is being used for fraud detection and risk management. In manufacturing, machine learning is being used for predictive maintenance and quality control.

16.   Blockchain: Unveiling the Potential of Decentralized Systems

Blockchain has gained a lot of attention in recent years due to its potential to create decentralized systems that are secure and transparent.

Introduction to Blockchain: Advantages and Disadvantages

Blockchain is a distributed ledger that stores data in a decentralized way. It is secure, transparent, and can be used to build decentralized applications. However, it is also expensive, slow, and energy-intensive.

Smart Contracts: Simplifying Business Processes

Smart contracts are self-executing contracts that are stored on the blockchain. They are used to automate business processes and ensure secure and transparent transactions.

Choosing the Right Blockchain Platform for Your Project

There are several blockchain platforms available, such as Ethereum, Hyperledger, and Corda. Choosing the right platform for your project depends on factors like scalability, security, and interoperability.

4. Internet of Things (IoT): A New Era of Programming

Introduction to IoT: Connecting Devices and Data

The Internet of Things (IoT) refers to a network of physical devices, sensors, and other objects that are connected to the Internet and can exchange data with each other. This technology has made it possible to create smart homes, smart cities, and various other interconnected systems that improve our daily lives.

Programming Languages for IoT: Choosing the Right One

IoT devices require specialized programming languages to function correctly. The most commonly used languages for IoT programming include C, Java, Python, and Node.js. Each language has its strengths and weaknesses, and developers must choose the right language based on the device's requirements and functionality.

Challenges and Solutions for IoT Programming

IoT programming involves several challenges, such as device compatibility issues, network security, and data management. To overcome these challenges, developers need to consider various factors such as device lifespan, power usage, and data processing. They must also ensure that the devices they create are compatible with other IoT devices and networks.

14.   Language Comparison: Which Programming Language to Choose?

C++, Java, Python, or Kotlin: Which Language to Choose for Your Project?

Choosing the right programming language for your project can be a daunting task. C++, Java, Python, and Kotlin are some of the most commonly used languages in the tech industry. C++ is ideal for systems programming, Java is suitable for enterprise-level applications, Python is perfect for data analysis and machine learning, and Kotlin is excellent for developing Android applications.

Factors to Consider When Choosing a Programming Language

When choosing a programming language, several factors come into play, including the project's scope and size, development time, budget, and the team's expertise. Developers must also consider the language's compatibility with other technologies, frameworks, and libraries.

4. Future of Programming: What's Next in the Tech Industry?

Quantum Computing and Its Impact on Programming

Quantum computing has the potential to revolutionize the tech industry. Quantum computers can solve problems faster than classical computers and perform complex operations that are impossible to achieve with traditional computers. As a result, quantum programming is becoming increasingly popular among developers.

Augmented Reality and Virtual Reality: The Future of User Interface

Augmented reality (AR) and virtual reality (VR) are becoming more commonplace in various industries, from gaming to healthcare. These technologies require specialized programming skills to develop immersive user interfaces that enhance the user experience.

Cloud Computing: The Future of Software Development and Deployment

Cloud computing has revolutionized software development and deployment. It offers scalable and cost-effective solutions for building and deploying applications. With the rise of cloud-based technologies, developers must have the necessary skills to create and deploy applications in the cloud.

13.	Conclusion: Embracing the Changing Landscape of Programming

Adapting to Emerging Trends and Technologies in Programming

As the tech industry continues to evolve, programmers must adapt to emerging trends and technologies to stay relevant and competitive. Learning new programming languages, frameworks, and libraries is crucial for developers to remain at the forefront of the industry.

Continued Learning and Development as a Programmer

Continued learning and development are essential for programmers to improve their skills, stay competitive, and remain relevant. From attending conferences to online courses and workshops, there are numerous resources available to help programmers enhance their knowledge and expertise. In conclusion, the programming landscape is changing rapidly, and keeping up with the latest trends and technologies is essential for developers to remain relevant and competitive. The emergence of new languages and technologies such as Rust, machine learning, blockchain, and IoT presents exciting opportunities for programmers to create innovative solutions and solve complex problems. As the tech industry continues to evolve, programmers need to keep learning and developing their skills to stay ahead of the game. By embracing the changing landscape of programming, we can unlock endless possibilities and shape the future of the industry.

FAQ

What is Rust?

Rust is a modern systems programming language that aims to provide fast execution combined with safety. It is designed to offer low-level control and performance while preventing common programming errors like null pointer exceptions and buffer overflows.

What is machine learning and why is it important in programming?

Machine learning is a type of artificial intelligence that involves training computer algorithms to learn from data and improve their performance over time. This technology has many applications in programming, such as in natural language processing, image recognition, and predictive analytics. Machine learning is important because it allows programmers to build intelligent systems that can make decisions and predictions based on data, which can be valuable in many industries.

What is blockchain and how can it be used in programming?

Blockchain is a decentralized ledger technology that allows for secure, transparent, and tamper-proof transactions. It can be used in programming to create applications that require a high level of security and trust, such as financial transactions, supply chain management, and voting systems. Blockchain is also being used to develop smart contracts, which are self-executing contracts with the terms of the agreement between buyer and seller being directly written into lines of code.

What are the benefits of learning multiple programming languages?

Learning multiple programming languages can be beneficial for several reasons. First, it allows programmers to have a broader understanding of different programming paradigms and techniques. This can help them solve problems more efficiently and creatively. Second, it can make programmers more versatile and adaptable, as they can switch between languages depending on the project or task at hand. Finally, learning multiple programming languages can make programmers more marketable and increase their job opportunities.

Programming is a constantly evolving field, and the role of programmers has changed significantly in recent years. Today, programmers are not just responsible for writing code but are expected to collaborate with other professionals and contribute to the development of a product or service. In this context, continuous learning is a vital component for programmers to keep up with the latest trends and technologies. This article discusses the evolving role of programmers and the importance of continuous learning in programming. We'll explore the benefits of continuous learning, strategies for effective learning, and the need for a balanced skill set that includes both technical and non-technical skills. Additionally, we'll discuss emerging trends and predictions for the future of programming and the evolving role of programmers in this field.

THE CHANGING LANDSCAPE OF PROGRAMMING: AN OVERVIEW

Introduction

Programming has come a long way since its inception in the mid-1800s. From punch cards to modern-day programming languages, this field has witnessed significant evolution. The continual advancement of technology has redefined the role of programmers, who are no longer just coding machines. They are now problem solvers, innovators, and collaborators who work closely with other professionals to create complex solutions.

The Historical Evolution of Programming

The first computer program was written in 1843 by Ada Lovelace, a computer pioneer. Programming languages like FORTRAN, COBOL, and assembly language were developed in the 1950s and 1960s. The rise of the internet led to the development of web-based languages such as HTML, CSS, and JavaScript. The current era is characterized by more sophisticated languages and frameworks like Python, Ruby, Angular, and React.

The Current State of Programming

Programming today has evolved from a solitary task to a group effort. Programmers no longer work in isolation, but rather collaborate, share knowledge, and work in teams. Also, there is an increasing emphasis on soft skills such as communication, problem-solving, and critical thinking. The modern-day programmer is expected to be well-rounded, with a mix of technical and interpersonal skills.

THE EXPANDING ROLE OF PROGRAMMERS: FROM CODING TO COLLABORATING

The Traditional Role of Programmers

Traditionally, the role of programmers was limited to writing code and fixing errors. They would work independently, and their job was to ensure that the code they wrote worked as intended. However, programming has evolved, and so has the role of programmers.

The New Role of Programmers

The modern-day programmer is involved in the entire software development cycle, from requirements gathering and design to testing and deployment. Programmers are problem solvers who work with other professionals to develop solutions that meet specific business needs. In addition to writing code, modern-day programmers are involved in planning, collaboration, and communication.

Collaboration in Programming: Teamwork and Communication Skills

While technical skills are still vital, collaboration and communication skills have become increasingly important in programming. Programmers must collaborate with designers, project managers, and end-users to identify and address business problems. Effective communication skills are critical to ensure that everyone is on the same page, and the project is delivered on time and within budget.

CONTINUOUS LEARNING: A VITAL COMPONENT FOR PROGRAMMERS

The Need for Continuous Learning

Continuous learning is crucial for programmers to stay up-to-date with the latest technologies and industry trends. Programming languages and frameworks continually evolve, and it's essential to keep up with these changes to remain relevant in the industry. Continuous learning not only ensures the programmer's job security but also keeps them motivated and engaged in their work.

The Benefits of a Lifelong Learning Mindset

Adopting a lifelong learning mindset has numerous benefits for programmers. It enables them to stay current, learn new skills, and broaden their knowledge base. Continuous learning also enhances problem-solving abilities, critical thinking, and decision-making skills. Additionally, it can lead to increased job satisfaction and career growth opportunities.

Obstacles to Continuous Learning

Continuous learning can be challenging, especially for programmers with busy schedules. Keeping up with the latest technologies can be overwhelming, and finding the time and resources to learn can be difficult. However, there are various avenues for learning, such as online courses, coding boot camps, and conferences. Programmers can also make time for learning by breaking down their learning goals into smaller, manageable tasks.

THE BENEFITS OF CONTINUOUS LEARNING FOR PROGRAMMERS AND ORGANIZATIONS

Improved Job Performance

Continuous learning enables programmers to stay up-to-date with the latest technologies and industry practices. This knowledge can be applied to their work, leading to improved job performance, increased efficiency, and higher quality work.

Increased Job Opportunities and Career Growth

Programmers who continually learn and develop new skills are more likely to be considered for new opportunities and promotions. Continuous learning opens up new career paths, enabling programmers to move into more advanced roles, such as team leads, architects, or project managers.

Better Business Outcomes for Organizations

Organizations that invest in continuous learning for their programming teams can reap significant benefits. These teams are more likely to be innovative, produce higher-quality work, and improve business outcomes. Additionally, continuous learning can lead to increased employee retention, job satisfaction, and motivation.

DISCUSSING THE EVOLVING ROLE OF PROGRAMMERS AND THE IMPORTANCE OF CONTINUOUS LEARNING

STRATEGIES FOR EFFECTIVE CONTINUOUS LEARNING IN PROGRAMMING

Continuous learning is not only important but essential for programmers to stay updated with the latest technologies and programming languages. Here are a few strategies for effective continuous learning in programming:

Setting Learning Goals and Objectives

Before starting any learning activity, it's crucial to set clear learning goals and objectives. Having a defined learning goal helps to stay focused, and motivated, and measure progress. For example, a programmer might set a goal to learn a new programming language or to develop a specific skill set in a particular area.

Choosing Appropriate Learning Methods

The learning method should be tailored to the specific learning goal and individual learning style. Some programmers prefer self-study through online courses, tutorial videos, or books, while others prefer hands-on learning through workshops, hackathons, or pair programming. Experimenting with different learning methods can help to find the most effective one.

Making Time for Learning

Making time for learning can be a challenge, especially for programmers who have a demanding workload. However, setting aside specific times for learning, prioritizing learning activities, and making learning a habit can help to overcome these challenges. Additionally, incorporating learning activities into daily work routines can also be helpful, such as using lunch breaks or downtime to read articles or watch tutorials.

THE IMPORTANCE OF SOFT SKILLS IN THE EVOLVING ROLE OF PROGRAMMERS

In addition to technical skills, soft skills are becoming increasingly important in the evolving role of programmers.

Definition of Soft Skills

Soft skills are interpersonal skills, including communication, teamwork, problem-solving, adaptability, creativity, and critical thinking.

The Importance of Soft Skills for Programmers

Soft skills are essential for programmers to work effectively in teams, communicate with stakeholders, and solve complex problems. In today's work environment, programmers are expected to have a broad range of skills, both technical and non-technical, to be successful in their roles.

Developing Soft Skills for Programmers

Developing soft skills can be challenging but is achievable through deliberate practice, feedback, and self-reflection. Additionally, seeking out opportunities to work on soft skills, such as volunteer work, mentoring, or public speaking, can help to develop these skills.

BALANCING TECHNICAL AND NON-TECHNICAL SKILLS: A CHALLENGE FOR MODERN PROGRAMMERS

The challenge for modern programmers is to balance technical and non-technical skills.

Technical and Non-Technical Skills: A Comparison

Technical skills are specific to programming languages, frameworks, and tools, while non-technical skills are interpersonal skills, such as communication, teamwork, and problem-solving.

The Need for a Balanced Skill Set

A balanced skill set is essential for programmers to be successful in their roles. Technical skills are necessary to develop and maintain software, while non-technical skills are essential for collaboration, communication, and problem-solving.

Challenges and Strategies for Balancing Technical and Non-Technical Skills

The challenge for programmers is to find a balance between technical and non-technical skills. One strategy is to seek out opportunities to develop non-technical skills through workshops, training programs, or peer mentoring. Additionally, finding ways to incorporate non-technical skills into daily work routines, such as practicing effective communication with team members or practicing problem-solving techniques, can also be helpful.

THE FUTURE OF PROGRAMMING: TRENDS AND PREDICTIONS FOR THE EVOLVING ROLE OF PROGRAMMERS

The field of programming is constantly evolving, and programmers need to stay updated with emerging technologies and paradigms.

Emerging Technologies and Paradigms

Emerging technologies and paradigms in programming include artificial intelligence, blockchain, serverless architecture, and the internet of Things (IoT). These emerging technologies and paradigms are changing the way applications are developed and deployed.

The Role of Programmers in Emerging Technologies

The role of programmers in emerging technologies is to understand the technology, develop and deploy applications, and solve complex problems that arise with the technology's implementation.

Future Challenges and Opportunities for Programmers

Future challenges for programmers include keeping up with rapidly evolving technologies, developing a broad range of skills, and collaborating with teams across different disciplines. The opportunities for programmers include developing innovative solutions, addressing complex problems, and contributing to the growth and development of emerging technologies. In conclusion, programming is a dynamic field, and its evolution demands a shift in the role of programmers. Continuous learning is a vital part of this change, and it offers many benefits to both programmers and organizations. By keeping up with the latest trends, developing soft skills, and balancing their technical and non-technical skills, programmers can position themselves for success in the future. With new technologies and paradigms emerging all the time, the role of programmers will continue to evolve, and it will be exciting to see what the future holds for this dynamic field.

FREQUENTLY ASKED QUESTIONS (FAQ)

Why is continuous learning important for programmers?

Continuous learning is essential for programmers to stay up-to-date with the latest trends and technologies. The field of programming is continuously evolving, and new tools, languages, and frameworks are emerging all the time. Programmers who don't keep up with the latest developments risk falling behind and becoming irrelevant in the job market. Continuous learning also helps programmers to improve their job performance, increase their job opportunities, and achieve career growth.

What are the benefits of soft skills for programmers?

Soft skills are crucial for programmers, especially as their role expands beyond writing code. Collaboration, teamwork, communication, and problem-solving skills are necessary for programmers to work effectively with other professionals, such as project managers, designers, and quality assurance engineers. Strong soft skills can help programmers build better relationships with their peers, improve project outcomes, and advance in their careers.

How can programmers balance their technical and non-technical skills?

Balancing technical and non-technical skills can be a challenge for programmers, but it's necessary for their success in the field. To achieve a balanced skill set, programmers can focus on developing both technical and non-technical skills, setting learning goals and objectives, and choosing appropriate learning methods. Additionally, they can seek feedback from their peers, mentors, and managers to identify areas for improvement and stay on track.

What are some emerging trends and paradigms in programming?

Several emerging trends and paradigms are shaping the future of programming. These include artificial intelligence (AI) and machine learning, blockchain, Internet of Things (IoT), and serverless computing. Programmers who specialize in these areas will likely have excellent job opportunities in the future. Additionally, the rise of low-code and no-code development platforms may change the way we think about programming, as it reduces the need for traditional coding skills.

Proven coding practices, tips, and techniques for writing clean, efficient, and maintainable code.

As a programmer, writing clean, efficient, and maintainable code is essential for producing software that is reliable and easy to work with. However, achieving these goals is not always easy. It requires adherence to best practices, continual learning and improvement, and a willingness to invest time and effort into writing quality code. In this article, we will explore proven coding practices, tips, and techniques for writing clean, efficient, and maintainable code. Whether you are a beginner or an experienced developer, these strategies will help you improve the quality of your code and become a better programmer.

INTRODUCTION TO WRITING CLEAN, EFFICIENT, AND MAINTAINABLE CODE

Writing clean, efficient, and maintainable code is essential for software development teams. Clean code is easy to read, understand, and modify. Efficient code is optimized for performance and resource consumption. Maintainable code is easy to modify and adapt to changing requirements. This article provides tips, practices, and techniques for coding clean, efficient, and maintainable software.

Why Writing Clean Code Matters

Clean code matters because it reduces the complexity and cost of software development. Clean code is easy to understand, modify, and troubleshoot. It reduces the likelihood of bugs, errors, and issues that can affect user experience and productivity. Clean code also promotes collaboration among developers and improves the overall quality of the software.

What Makes Code Efficient and Maintainable

Efficient code is optimized for performance, speed, and resource consumption. It uses minimal resources and completes tasks quickly. Efficient code is also scalable, meaning it can handle larger workloads and adapt to changing requirements. Maintainable code is easy to maintain and modify. It uses a modular design that enables developers to make changes without affecting other parts of the codebase. It is also easy to troubleshoot and diagnose problems.

BEST CODING PRACTICES TO FOLLOW

Naming Conventions and Formatting Standards

Consistent naming conventions and formatting standards make code easier to read and understand. Use descriptive names for variables, functions, and classes that reflect their purpose and functionality. Consistent formatting of code also makes it easier to read and understand.

Appropriate Use of Comments and Documentation

Use comments and documentation to explain the purpose and functionality of the code. Comments should be concise and explain complex sections of code. Documentation should provide an overview of the codebase, its purpose, and how to use it.

Code Reusability and Modularity

Reusing code and creating modular code are essential practices for efficient and maintainable code. Create reusable functions and classes that can be used in multiple parts of the code. Use modular design principles to create self-contained modules that can be easily modified or replaced without affecting other parts of the code.

TIPS TO IMPROVE CODE EFFICIENCY

Minimizing Code Redundancy

Reducing code redundancy can significantly improve code efficiency. Remove duplicate code and consolidate similar functions into reusable code. This reduces the amount of code that needs to be executed and reduces the likelihood of errors.

Optimizing Loops and Control Structures

Optimizing loops and control structures can improve code performance. Use appropriate loop structures such as for loops and while loops. Use control structures such as if-else statements and switch statements where appropriate.

Using Appropriate Data Structures and Algorithms

Using appropriate data structures and algorithms is critical for efficient code. Use data structures such as arrays, lists, and maps that are appropriate for the task. Use appropriate algorithms for sorting, searching, and other tasks.

TECHNIQUES FOR WRITING MAINTAINABLE CODE

Writing Readable and Understandable Code

Writing readable and understandable code is essential for maintainability. Use clear and concise naming conventions and formatting standards. Use comments and documentation to explain the code's purpose and functionality.

Ensuring Code Scalability and Flexibility

Ensuring code scalability and flexibility can improve maintainability. Use modular design principles to create self-contained modules that can be easily modified or replaced without affecting other parts of the code. Use design patterns that promote flexibility and scalability.

Effective Error Handling and Exception Management

Effective error handling and exception management can improve maintainability. Use appropriate error-handling techniques to prevent crashes and unexpected behavior. Use exception management to handle errors gracefully and provide informative error messages.

STRATEGIES FOR DEBUGGING AND TROUBLESHOOTING CODE

When coding, it's inevitable that things will go wrong. While frustrating, bugs and errors are a natural part of the process. Luckily, there are strategies you can employ to make debugging and troubleshooting your code easier and more efficient.

Effective Debugging Techniques

One important technique for effective debugging is to isolate the problem. This involves breaking down the code into smaller parts to identify where the problem is originating. Another useful technique is to use print statements to track the flow of data through the code and identify where the error is occurring. Additionally, stepping through the code line by line with a debugger can help pinpoint the problem.

Debugging Tools and Resources

There are a variety of tools and resources available to help with debugging. Integrated development environments (IDEs) such as Visual Studio and Eclipse have built-in debuggers that allow you to step through your code. Online forums and communities like Stack Overflow can also be helpful in finding solutions to common problems.

Common Debugging Pitfalls and How to Avoid Them

One common pitfall in debugging is assuming the problem is where the error is being reported. It's important to trace the error back to its source and not just fix the symptom. Another mistake is not testing the fix thoroughly before declaring the problem solved. Finally, it's important to avoid debugging when you're tired or distracted, as this can lead to careless mistakes.

IMPORTANCE OF DOCUMENTATION IN CODE MAINTENANCE

Documentation is an essential part of code maintenance. Not only does it make it easier for others to understand your code, but it can also help you remember why you wrote the code in a particular way.

Why Code Documentation is Important

Code documentation helps make your code more understandable and maintainable. It allows other developers to work with your code and helps reduce the amount of time needed to understand the codebase. Additionally, documentation can help prevent bugs by clearly outlining the intended behavior of the code.

Types of Documentation and When to Use Them

There are several types of documentation, including comments within code, READMEs, and user guides. Comments within code can be used to explain complex code, while READMEs can provide an overview of the project and its purpose. User guides can help users understand how to use the software.

Best Practices for Documenting Code

When documenting code, it's important to use clear and concise language that's easily understandable. Additionally, it's important to update the documentation whenever changes are made to the code. Finally, documentation should be reviewed and updated periodically to ensure it remains accurate.

TOOLS AND RESOURCES FOR CODE OPTIMIZATION AND MAINTENANCE

Maintaining and optimizing code is an ongoing process. Luckily, there are a variety of tools and resources available to help make the process easier and more efficient.

Code Editors and IDEs for Efficient Coding

Code editors and IDEs can make coding more efficient by providing useful features such as auto-completion and syntax highlighting. Some popular code editors and IDEs include Visual Studio Code, Sublime Text, and IntelliJ IDEA.

Automated Testing and Code Quality Tools

Automated testing and code quality tools can help ensure your code meets certain standards and that there are no major bugs. Examples of such tools include JUnit, PHPUnit, and PyLint.

Collaboration and Version Control Tools for Code Maintenance

Version control tools like Git and SVN can help keep track of changes made to the code. Additionally, collaboration tools like GitHub and Bitbucket can help make it easier for developers to work together and manage changes to the codebase. In conclusion, writing clean, efficient, and maintainable code is a continuous process that requires dedication and effort. By following the proven coding practices, tips, and techniques outlined in this article, you can improve your coding skills and produce better software. Remember to always strive for simplicity, readability, and modularity in your code and to make use of the various tools and resources available to you. With time and practice, you can become a proficient programmer capable of producing high-quality code that is easy to work with and maintain.

FAQ

What are some common coding practices that can help me write cleaner code?

Some common coding practices that can help you write cleaner code include following appropriate naming conventions, adhering to formatting standards, and avoiding code redundancy. Additionally, writing comments and documentation regularly can help improve the readability and maintainability of your code.

How can I improve the efficiency of my code?

There are several strategies you can use to improve the efficiency of your code. These include minimizing code redundancy, optimizing loops and control structures, and using appropriate data structures and algorithms. Additionally, you can make use of profiling tools to identify performance bottlenecks in your code.

Why is code maintainability important?

The code maintainability is important because it helps ensure that software remains functional and reliable over time. When code is maintainable, it is easier to update and modify as requirements change, and it is less likely to contain bugs or other issues. This makes it easier for developers to work with the code and reduces the likelihood of errors or issues arising in production.

What tools and resources are available for code optimization and maintenance?

There are a variety of tools and resources available for code optimization and maintenance, including code editors and IDEs, automated testing and code quality tools, and collaboration and version control tools. Additionally, there are many online communities and forums where developers can ask questions, share knowledge, and collaborate with others to improve their coding skills.

Recommended resources, including books, online tutorials, and communities for further learning and growth.

Continuous learning and self-improvement are essential for personal and professional growth. As we navigate through life and our careers, it is crucial to seek out resources that can help us expand our knowledge and skills. Fortunately, there are countless books, online tutorials, and communities available to those who are looking to learn and grow. In this article, we'll explore some of the top recommended resources for those who are seeking to further their education, acquire new skills, and connect with like-minded individuals. Whether you're a seasoned professional or just starting, there's something here for everyone.

INTRODUCTION TO RECOMMENDED RESOURCES FOR PERSONAL AND PROFESSIONAL GROWTH

The journey of personal and professional growth is a never-ending one. With the constant changes and advancements in all fields, it's essential to stay on top of your game and continuously improve yourself. Fortunately, there are various resources available to help you achieve your goals, whether it be through books, online tutorials, or networking groups. In this article, we'll be exploring some of the recommended resources to aid you in your continuous learning and self-improvement.

TOP BOOKS FOR CONTINUOUS LEARNING AND SELF-IMPROVEMENT

Books have always been a valuable source of knowledge and inspiration. Whether you're looking for new perspectives, self-help techniques, or industry insights, there's a book out there to meet your needs. Below are some of the top books for continuous learning and self-improvement.

Classics that stand the test of time

- How to Win Friends and Influence People by Dale Carnegie

- The 7 Habits of Highly Effective People by Stephen R. Covey

- Think and Grow Rich by Napoleon Hill

- The Alchemist by Paulo Coelho

- The Power of Now by Eckhart Tolle

Recent releases making waves in the industry

- Atomic Habits by James Clear

- Mindset: The New Psychology of Success by Carol Dweck

- The Four Hour Work Week by Timothy Ferriss

- The Lean Startup by Eric Ries

- Essentialism: The Disciplined Pursuit of Less by Greg McKeown

Books for specific industries or niches

- Creativity, Inc. by Ed Catmull (for the film and animation industry)

- The Design of Everyday Things by Don Norman (for the UX and product design industry)

- The Phoenix Project by Gene Kim, Kevin Behr, and George Spafford (for the IT and DevOps industry)

- Start with Why by Simon Sinek (for the leadership and management industry)

- The Innovator's Dilemma by Clayton Christensen (for the innovation and entrepreneurship industry)

ONLINE TUTORIALS AND COURSES FOR EXPANDING YOUR KNOWLEDGE AND SKILLS

In today's digital age, online tutorials and courses are a great way to expand your knowledge and skills. There are various options available, from free resources to paid courses that offer certifications. Below are some of the recommended online tutorials and courses for expanding your knowledge and skills.

Free and paid options for online learning

- Khan Academy

- Udemy

- Coursera

- edX

- Skillshare

Established online course providers

- LinkedIn Learning

- Udacity

- Pluralsight

- Lynda.com

- Codecademy

Online tutorials and courses for specific skills or industries

- Adobe Creative Cloud courses on Skillshare

- Data Science courses on Coursera

- Google Analytics Academy

- Hubspot Academy for digital marketing courses

- AWS Training and Certification for cloud computing courses

COMMUNITIES AND NETWORKING GROUPS FOR CONNECTING WITH LIKE-MINDED INDIVIDUALS

Networking and interacting with like-minded individuals is an excellent way to stay motivated and learn from others' experiences. Joining communities and groups that share similar interests can also provide you with valuable insights and opportunities. Below are some of the recommended communities and networking groups for connecting with like-minded individuals.

Professional networking groups

- LinkedIn Groups

- Business Networking International (BNI)

- Toastmasters International

- International Association of Business Communicators (IABC)

- Young Entrepreneur Council (YEC)

Online communities and forums

- Reddit

- GrowthHackers

- Product Hunt

- Hacker News

- Indie Hackers

Meetup groups and events

- Meetup.com

- Eventbrite

- Startup Grind

- Creative Mornings

- Women in Technology International (WITI)

FREE RESOURCES FOR LEARNING AND GROWTH ON A BUDGET

Learning and personal growth shouldn't have to come with a hefty price tag. Fortunately, there are plenty of free resources available online that can help you expand your knowledge and improve your skills. Here are some of the best resources for learning and growth on a budget:

Online libraries and databases

Many public libraries offer free online access to a wide range of resources, including eBooks, audiobooks, and academic journals. Online databases like JSTOR and Project MUSE offer access to scholarly articles and research papers. By taking advantage of these resources, you can access valuable information without spending a dime.

Free webinars and podcasts

Webinars and podcasts are a great way to learn from experts in your field, and there are plenty of free options available. Websites like TED Talks and Coursera offer free lectures and courses, while many industry-specific websites offer free webinars regularly. By tuning in to these free resources, you can gain valuable insights and knowledge from experts, without breaking the bank.

Open-source software and tools

Many software programs and tools are available as open-source, meaning they are free for anyone to use and modify. This is particularly useful for individuals looking to learn new programming languages or software development skills. Websites like GitHub offer a wide range of open-source projects and tools to explore.

SPECIALIZED RESOURCES FOR NICHE INDUSTRIES AND INTERESTS

Depending on your field of interest or industry, there may be specialized resources available that can help you develop your skills and knowledge even further. Here are some examples of resources specific to different industries:

Resources for creative industries

Creative professionals can benefit from visiting websites like Behance and Dribbble, which showcase portfolios and designs from other creatives. There are also free design software options like Canva and GIMP that offer tools and templates to help with graphic design projects.

Resources for tech and IT industries

Tech professionals can benefit from resources like Codecademy and Udacity, which offer courses and tutorials on coding and software development. GitHub is also a valuable resource for coding and software development projects.

Resources for healthcare and wellness industries

Those in the healthcare and wellness industries can benefit from websites like PubMed and WebMD, which offer free access to research and medical information. There are also website and app options like MyFitnessPal and Headspace that promote wellness practices and healthy living habits.

TIPS FOR SELECTING THE RIGHT RESOURCES FOR YOUR LEARNING GOALS

With so many resources available, it can be overwhelming to choose the right ones for your learning goals. Here are some tips to help you narrow down your options:

Assessing your learning style and preferences

Consider your learning style and preferences when selecting resources. For example, if you're a visual learner, you may prefer video-based tutorials over written guides.

Considering the credibility and relevance of resources

Ensure the resources you select come from reputable sources and are relevant to your field or interests. Look for resources with high ratings and reviews, or recommendations from trusted colleagues or mentors.

Setting specific learning goals and finding resources to match

Set specific learning goals for yourself, and then search for resources that match those goals. For example, if you're looking to improve your public speaking skills, look for resources that specifically focus on that topic.

CONCLUSION AND FINAL THOUGHTS ON THE IMPORTANCE OF ONGOING EDUCATION AND GROWTH

In today's fast-paced and ever-changing world, ongoing education and growth are essential for personal and professional success. By taking advantage of the many resources available, you can continue to expand your knowledge and skills, improve your career prospects, and enhance your personal growth and development. Whether you choose free resources or invest in specialized training, the key is to never stop learning. In conclusion, the resources outlined in this article are just a starting point for your journey toward ongoing education and growth. There are countless options available, and the key is to find the ones that best suit your needs and learning style. Investing in your personal and professional development is a lifelong process that requires dedication and commitment. With the help of these recommended resources and your initiative, you can continue to learn and improve for years to come.

FAQ

What if I am on a tight budget, are there any free resources available?

Absolutely! There are several free resources available for those who are on a budget. Online libraries, open-source tools and software, and free webinars and podcasts are just a few examples. We've included a section in this article specifically dedicated to free resources for learning and growth.

How do I know if an online course or tutorial is credible?

It's important to do your research before investing time and money into an online course or tutorial. Look for reviews and testimonials from other users, check the credentials of the instructor or provider, and make sure the content aligns with your learning goals. We've included some tips in this article for selecting the right resources for your learning goals.

What if I prefer in-person learning and connection, are there any resources available for me?

Absolutely! There are several meetup groups and events that offer in-person learning and connection opportunities. We've included a section in this article on communities and networking groups for connecting with like-minded individuals.

I'm not sure where to start, are there any all-in-one resources available?

There are several all-in-one resources available, such as online learning platforms that offer a wide range of courses and tutorials. We've included some established online course providers in this article that may be a good starting point. Additionally, it's important to assess your learning style and preferences to determine which resources are the best fit for you.